PASTA, PASTA, PASTA!

Spaghetti, macaroni, rigatoni, vermicelli . . . everyone loves pasta. It's fun to eat, inexpensive, and quick and easy to cook. The only trouble is, it's fattening. Right? *Wrong!*

Let Elisa Celli show you how real, Italian-made pasta is one of the best diet foods in the world. *The Pasta Diet* gives you:

- Over 100 recipes for main dishes, dips and sauces, salad dressings, side dishes, special pasta meals for entertaining, and more
- Pasta cooking tips including ways to save time, how to buy and store fresh herbs, choosing the right cheeses, oil, and wines, and much more
- Calorie amounts per serving for each dish.

"It contains many good recipes for pasta and other foods. You don't have to be dieting to enjoy this cookbook."
—*News American* (Baltimore)

ELISA CELLI is a well-known food consultant, gourmet writer, and critic. She has operated a chain of cooking schools, acts as a food consultant to a number of New York City restaurants, and is the founder of Creative Gourmet Enterprises, where she teaches cooking. A highly respected film actress as well, Elisa has appeared in a number of major motion pictures, and has many celebrity friends who have lost weight on her diet.

the PASTA DIET

ELISA CELLI

WARNER BOOKS

A Warner Communications Company

WARNER BOOKS EDITION

Book design by H. Roberts Design

Cover design by Barbara Buck

Warner Books, Inc.
75 Rockefeller Plaza
New York, N.Y. 10019

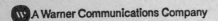 A Warner Communications Company

Printed in the United States of America

This book was originally published in hardcover,
by Warner Books

First Mass Market Paperback Printing: August, 1985

10 9 8 7 6 5 4 3 2 1

Acknowledgments

My appreciation and *molte grazie*

To God for giving me so much . . . and now letting me "give back" through my writings, which help people become healthier and happier.

To My Beautiful Familia: my fabulous Mamma, Adelaida D'Antony, who taught me so much about life and especially about classic Italian cooking; my brothers, Lou, Joe, and Bob (Luigi, Guiseppe, and Roberto) for their help always; my husband, Trevor Wallace, ever supportive, who painlessly and happily lost 54 pounds on my pasta diet and is still enjoying pasta and wine. A super talent in his own right— writer, producer, and director of many well-known motion pictures and television programs and more to come. Bravo!

Contents

Foreword
By: J. Estrada, M.D.

I heard about the Pasta Diet a while back when I first met Elisa Celli at a small social gathering. Passing down a banquet table, I was about to reach for some greasy dollop of a meatball with a thick, gooey portion of what looked like spaghetti when someone stayed my hand. "Take it from me," a voice cautioned me gently, "don't eat that. You don't need it and it's not good for you."

We doctors do not ordinarily get advice of this sort. We are in the habit of dispensing it, particularly on the subject of food. It's also true, however, that on the subject of nutrition we are not as thoroughly trained as most people think. I was curious why the charming lady, who introduced herself as Elisa Celli, would be so anxious about that hearty portion I had heaped onto my plate.

"I love Italian food," I objected defensively.

"But that's as Italian as Eskimo Pie," Elisa Celli said. She took the plate from me and brought another. "Now try this," she urged. It had been made by her own hand, she assured me, and it was Italian as her own mama.

She served me a portion of pasta with a creamy sauce and freshly cooked vegetables. Compared to the spaghetti and meatball I'd just put aside it looked as light as air and immensely appetizing.

Miss Celli informed me that the delightful treat I had just consumed was called Pasta Primavera and that it had been taken from her own repertoire of low-calorie Italian dishes—*real* Italian cooking, she stressed, not to be confused with the terribly fattening, nutritionally unbalanced Italian-American variety all of us know so well.

During the next half hour I listened to an inspiring lecture in which I was astonished to hear Miss Celli refer to her pasta-based dishes as "diet food." She herself, with her marvelous slim figure, definitely offered the best testimonial to the virtues of the "thin" Italian kitchen of which she was such an enthusiastic champion.

For one thing, I learned that there are different kinds of pasta—the wrong type which *is* fattening, and the right Italian kind, of which you can eat normal portions and lose weight rapidly or slowly, according to the dieter's own requirements. I also learned that pasta lends itself literally to untold combinations with vegetables, meats, and sauces. And, what was new to me, I discovered the economical side of the Pasta Diet, its low cost in time and money.

I learned more as Elisa Celli sent me the recipes she was gathering for presentation in this book. And some research on my part further revealed that she had not exaggerated when she called the Pasta Diet a "nutritional miracle," containing all the necessary complex carbohydrates, protein, vitamins, and minerals one needs.

Medically it is by now well established that rapid weight loss is best achieved by a diet based on carbohydrates rather than one rich in protein. The carbohydrates contained in pasta meet the body's metabolic needs better than the protein-rich diets which were in fashion some years ago. Carbohydrates yield greater appetite satisfaction than protein; furthermore, protein-rich diets are often accompanied by side effects which have proven to be harmful. The Pasta Diet is low in cholesterol, and it can only be beneficial to the arteries which may have been long clogged by dietary malpractices involving protein.

As a doctor and a devotee of this marvelous way of Italian cooking, I can recommend the Pasta Diet to all those who seek to lose weight in a safe, sound, and responsible manner.

Introduction

Until I proved the success of my Pasta Diet, people did not believe it. Could you slim down while you enjoyed a plate of pasta with a delicious sauce of clams, calamari, or shrimp, enriched by the zest of tomato and the piquancy of herbs? This delicate sauce of ricotta cheese with mushroom and herbs—could it really be *diet food?* That exciting pesto sauce—would it really help lose unwanted pounds?

Yes, yes, and yes again! It may be hard to believe, but the gastronomic delights you'll encounter in the menu program of this book average only between 220 to 380 calories each! That's fewer calories than a ho-hum sandwich or a boring steak.

The Pasta Diet is based on the Italian way of eating adapted to the weight-conscious American. It includes food so good that for the first time losing weight becomes remarkably easy. The Pasta Diet is not a regimen, it's a *festa* complete with wine . . . and even luscious Italian desserts!

The effectiveness of my Pasta Diet has been proven in some of the most expensive spas in Europe and America. I've demonstrated it in restaurants and on talk shows all across the country. It's been adopted by the stars of stage and screen for whom losing weight and maintaining figures are essential.

I well recall how pleased I was when Dolly Parton enthused about my diet in a *People* magazine interview—she said it had saved her career. Her frequent traveling was playing havoc with her eating habits. Two years ago, before doing a movie, she went on my Pasta Diet and lost 24 pounds without any effort at all.

Dolly Parton discovered, as you will, how easy it is to follow my quick and delectable recipes. She could whip up her favorite spaghetti with mushroom sauce in a matter of minutes. On the movie set, however, she had to make larger batches—so many of the crew members rapidly became converts to the Pasta Diet, for this unique Italian way of dieting.is unlike any other diet.

It not only promises a weight loss of up to ten pounds in two weeks for those who wish to shed their excess pounds rapidly, but it is also an unsurpassable way to maintain your weight on a lifetime eating program that keeps the pounds off permanently.

The Italians have stayed slim and healthy on the same diet for centuries. You can, too.

Here's to the *festa! Fantastico!*

Join the Trend Toward Lighter Cooking, Say, "Pasta, Please!"

For the past fifteen years I have had a mission.

I've been trying to persuade people that there is an ideal way to lose weight—up to ten pounds in two weeks—and that they can maintain their figures and always stay slim. What's more, I've been telling them that they can achieve this goal by feasting on one of the world's great cuisines. And further, that it provides the soundest nutrition.

I've been telling them to eat Italian food.

I can almost see you shaking your head.

And I don't blame you. For what the average American thinks is Italian food is really *American*-Italian food: doughy pizza, sauces you can cut with a knife, greasy meatballs, canned spaghetti, heavy oils, and all kinds of fried foods.

Though I grew up in an Italian home, no one ever offered me such fare. I can recall only the joy of meals that were scant in calories and rich in taste: fresh vegetables, scrumptious seafood, delicious poultry and meats, delicate spices, the natural sweetness of fresh fruit, the fine tang of wine . . . and the exciting magic of pasta.

Pasta?

Yes, PASTA!

Lots and lotsa pasta!!!

Pasta in all its flavorful and wholesome varieties of wheat and spinach! Pasta in all its different shapes and sizes! Pasta in sauces or pasta in broth! Pasta that keeps you slim, healthy, and full of pep! Pasta at least once a day.

In our large family we must have eaten tons of pasta; yet all the women in our house had figures like the proverbial hourglass, and the men were slim and strong. In fact, in the little village in the Abruzzi where I was born I do not recall seeing many overweight people, though pasta was the staple in the diet for all. These villagers actually ate twice as much as my American friends—but they did not gain an ounce!

THE LIVING PROOF

My mission to convert Americans to the Pasta Diet has been rewarding first of all to myself. While keeping me trim all my life, it has allowed me to indulge in my favorite food. As I pursued my pasta education, I went traveling to Italy, Switzerland, and New York, where I learned to perfect my *cucina magra*, the thin cuisine Italian-style. I had the satisfaction of seeing people shed weight, look more attractive, and feel better, both physically and psychologically, in the health spas that adopted my Pasta Diet. And the diet brought me together with a lot of wonderful men and women in the film, television, and restaurant world.

Being an actress myself, I've spent a lot of time around people to whom "watch your weight" was the first commandment. Celebrities can't afford to put their precious figures in jeopardy by eating fattening foods that are unhealthy, yet their demanding schedules call for fast energy and allow little time to prepare an entire meal.

For many of them, pasta has been the miraculous solution, and it is now regularly eaten by actors and actresses, models and athletes. They've discovered that pasta is an ideal and effective "shedder of weight"—*and* that it has the taste to satisfy gourmets, the energy to charge hours of strenuous activity, and the nutrition to safeguard your health as well as being fantastically easy to prepare. (A serving of pasta is ready in a matter of minutes.)

My pasta recipes have found favor with such marvelous performers as Sophia Loren, Gina Lollabrigida, Robert De Niro, Dolly Parton, Liza Minnelli, Cheryl Tiegs, Richard Chamberlain, Linda Evans, Bernadette Peters, and Brooke Shields. My recipes have been used to highlight festive dinners or to provide an escape from the cottage cheese-salad routine by Bob Hope, Dinah Shore, Danny Kaye, Johnny Carson, Angie Dickinson, Frank Sinatra, and many, many others.

I became a diet and gourmet cooking consultant for entertainment figures quite by accident. My roles in films such as *The Godfather*, *The French Connection*, and *Death Wish* may not have been the most memorable (I always wore a wig!), but on location, people remembered my performances at the kitchen range. "Hey, Elisa, where's the pasta?" was a question I heard over and over.

What intrigued the actors and actresses with whom I worked and socialized was simply how I managed to stay slim and eat so much pasta! They listened when I talked about the role of wine with and in my meals. And they were eager to discover how in the world I managed to cook four-course dinners in 15 or 20 minutes. It never took me long to persuade them of the virtues of the Pasta Diet.

They saw in me the living proof! And went on to indulge their appetites for pasta, pasta, pasta.

- A favorite recipe of Victoria Principal and James Garner is Pasta Primavera, a mixture of pasta and fresh vegetables.
- Everybody knows that Sophia Loren has a fabulous figure. But did you know that this beautiful woman dines regularly on spaghetti and other pastas?
- Frank Sinatra has probably the only kitchen built around pasta. His stove even has built-in pasta kettles.
- Dolly Parton lost a total of 24 pounds on the Pasta

Diet. The delightful varieties of pasta broke her
addiction to sweets and slabs of bread soaked in
butter!
- Liza Minnelli, though she had an Italian father and
  already possessed a wonderful understanding of food,
  slimmed down considerably by following the finer
  points of the *Pasta Diet*.
- Robert De Niro and Al Pacino saw the light about
  their steak-and-potato eating habits after learning how
  simple it is to squeeze the calories from spaghetti.

It's easy to see why the stars love pasta when you
consider, for instance, that the Pasta Primavera I whip up for
James Garner takes 15 minutes to prepare and contains about
250 calories.

The sauce I taught Brook Shields to make for her pasta
takes exactly 1 minute and contains practically no calories.
The sauce is a simple combination of tomatoes and basil. It
tastes divine!

These stars have discovered the secret of keeping slim
while dining on a variety of exciting pasta dishes night after
night.

The secret is the preparation.

American-style Italian food contains too much oil, butter,
and heavily floured pasta. Those ingredients will put pounds
on anyone!

But if the food is prepared in the true Italian tradition,
which requires a minimum of time to cook, the calories are
drastically reduced. A number of top spas in America, such
as Gurney's International Health and Beauty Spa in
Montauk, Long Island, regularly feature my Pasta Diet on a
succulent menu that enables patrons to lose up to ten
pounds in two weeks!

And you, too, can join the trend toward lighter cooking,
lighter eating, and lighter weight.

With this book you will be astonished to see how easy
and simple it is to enter that paradise where you can fill up
and slim down. All you need to do is follow the recipes and
say, "Pasta, please!"

THE PASTA DIET IS . . .

- Flexible in choices of food types
- Designed to fit into your lifestyle
- Ideal for losing weight quickly
- Perfect for "maintenance"-type eating, requiring only adjustments in portions, sauces, and the amount of wine consumed
- Based on a serving of pasta at least once a day

2

Losing Weight with the Food of the Eighties

Americans in the eighties are different. There are all sorts of statistics and studies to show how they differ from Americans in the past, but for me, the proof is the way they've taken to pasta.

More than one nutritionist or gourmet cook in recent years has hailed pasta as "the food of the eighties." They've waxed eloquent about its versatility, wholesomeness, economy, and zest. They've enumerated the qualities that make pasta so perfectly suited to the new American consciousness of weight, nutrition, health, and simplicity of cooking.

I share their enthusiasm to the fullest. My only question is, "Why did you wait so long?"

If you are still struggling with the idea that to lose weight you must forget about pasta, if you still say sadly, "I love Italian food, but I'm on a diet," the Pasta Diet is my gift to you.

THE PASTA DIET IS. . .

A nutritional program that is easy to live with at home, in restaurants, or when entertaining guests.

For so long, pasta has had "bad press." Americans felt that the mere thought of pasta would put pounds on their hips. Pasta acquired this sinister image not through any intrinsic fault, but because of the way Americans crudely smothered pasta's own inoffensive calories with butter, cream, and rich sauces.

The truth, however, as any well-informed Italian will tell you, is that *pasta is one of the least fattening foods you can eat!* That is, pasta as it is made, cooked, and served in Italy.

Today I am witnessing a happy event. The *real* pasta has come out of the closet. *One cup of cooked "al dente" (slightly chewy, the way it should be cooked) spaghetti or macaroni equals 155 calories—about the same as a tiny 3-ounce hamburger.* Americans have finally discovered the "amazing" fact . . .

You can eat pasta every day and lose weight!

WHAT IS PASTA?

Marco Polo is said to have brought pasta to Europe from his travels to China. I admire the intrepid Venetian and would be the last to deprive him of his noodles. But with all respect to Signor Polo, pasta was eaten in Italy long before he set out on his voyages to Cathay. An ancient Roman recipe actually calls for a form of fettucine with cheese, and there are other recipes which point to a long train of ancestors of Italy's national dish.

Naturally, a dish with such a long tradition behind it occupies a special place in the hearts of a people. Italians customarily offer awards to the best pasta creations. There are statues, and even museums, honoring the artful models made of pasta. Though the United States does not yet heap laurels on its pasta artists, this country is fast becoming one of the leading pasta producers. That is because this country ranks among the foremost growers of durum wheat, which goes into the making of the finest pasta.

Every Italian mama knows that the best pasta contains the greatest amount of durum wheat. This is the healthiest, lightest pasta you can eat, with firm texture and delicate flavor. The refined inner kernels of hard, durum wheat, ground into a semifine flour, produce the semolina which, mixed with water, becomes the dough that can be made into an incredible variety of dried pasta shapes (there are over 200!), spaghetti, macaroni, rigatoni, and vermicelli, to name only a few. When the flour is mixed with water and eggs a soft dough, which can be rolled out and cut into flat ribbons of varying widths, produces what we know as "noodles"—fettucine, linguine, tagliarini.

Besides its numerous shapes, pasta comes in five colors: the regular cream; a light-brown variety made with whole wheat flour; yellow, made with eggs (egg noodles); green, made with spinach; and the still somewhat rare red, made with tomato.

PASTA: AN APPETITE SUPPRESSANT!

All my life I have prepared, cooked, and eaten pasta and when people asked how I or other pasta devotees managed to stay so slim, I would answer them, "Italian pasta with the right sauces is not fattening." I was unaware of the scientific principles underlying the "slimming" properties of the pasta that kept me thin.

It was not until about five years ago that I began to study physiology, nutrition, and biochemistry as they related to our intake of food and how this food affects our health and well-being. For months I did nothing but pore over books and journals; I consulted long indexes and my library filled up with medical tomes; I sought out scientists and experts at universities and research centers, and I was fascinated with what I learned.

At the same time I found that I had been lagging behind the times. The popularity of pasta as "the food of the eighties," I discovered, had grown among people who were better educated about the subject than I was. A large number of Americans had become aware of the relationship between health, body weight, and nutrition. They chose pasta as their staple dish not just because it kept them thin and healthy but because, to use the words of a leading agricultural specialist, pasta happens to be a nutritional dream.

And why was pasta being honored with such extravagant praise? I had already found this out for myself. It was because of its *carbohydrates* and *fiber*, the two chief concerns of today's modern, up-to-date dieter.

WHAT IS THE MOST INTELLIGENT DIET?

It is one which *individualizes rather than generalizes.*
The Pasta Diet is not a mass diet; it does not insist on one food regimen for all.
The menus for weight loss are individualized nutritional programs, designed to fit an individual's particular needs and lifestyle.

Before Americans began to discover the considerable virtues of carbohydrates as both a reducing agent and a wholesome ingredient they paid a heavy price for their ignorance. They had generally been raised on high-protein foods: butter, cheese, meats, and loads of *refined* carbohydrates, such as white flour and sugar. That regimen, rich in fats and cholesterol and low in fiber, had led to all sorts of ailments, from fatigue, stress, and nausea to heart disease, diabetes, and arteriosclerosis. Millions of people learned enough about the dietary "time bombs" they were planting in their systems to begin questioning the food they were eating.

The real horror of the high-protein menu, however, was reserved for its primary victims: the overweight men and women who wanted to reduce. What had they turned to when they decided to shed fat? The very same high-protein, low-fiber foods they had been eating all along!

The new rationale was that proteins "burned" fat, a theory that has now been discredited by scientists and nutritionists as dangerous and erroneous. It was no coincidence that those who followed such diets were always warned by the promoters of those regimens not to stay on such a diet for more than two weeks. The reason? The body simply cannot use protein in this way *without carbohydrates.*

It has now been proved that no crash—or any other— diet can succeed without carbohydrates. One scientist believes that people have a "distinct hunger" for this nutritional element, and that failure to acknowledge our "craving for the carb" is, incidentally, one of the chief reasons why the popular protein diets never make good on their promises. Such diets don't work because they eliminate a highly valuable part of nutrition.

If you are on a diet and wish to lose up to ten pounds in two weeks you must first master one thing: your appetite. And the best appetite-suppressants, as has been conclusively shown, are carbohydrates.

A high-protein diet of, say, meat and fish still leaves you hungry and craving something sweet or starchy, because the meat and fish have not satisfied your body's need for carbohydrates. The "filled" feeling you get from eating a bowl of pasta is not accidental. That bowl of pasta has satisfied your metabolic need. As a result, you won't feel the "urge to splurge."

Another reason for the appetite-suppressing properties of carbohydrates is that unlike, for example, refined sugar, complex carbohydrates enter the bloodstream more slowly. This slow and steady absorption of carbohydrates eliminates the low blood sugar that sets up a desire for more sugar. In essence it shuts off the "appetite switch."

SAUCE! SAUCE! SAUCE!

Pasta is one of the world's most popular foods, and one of the reasons for this is the almost inexhaustible variety in which it can be served. There are an enormous number of sauces to match the hundreds of kinds of pasta, from the thinnest "angel hair" to the plumpest, curviest shells and bows. You can actually serve pasta every day of the year without duplicating a sauce. These endless combinations actually convinced me that Italy's national dish could be an American dieter's delight.

Let's face it, nothing is more intimidating to someone who wants to lose weight than having to subject his palate to a strict regimen of bland and tasteless diet food. Pasta, with its range of sauces, from the delicately subtle to the manfully robust, offers relief from the boring, regimented diets that make the mouth water for all the things it can't have. And what's more, a meal-sized portion tossed with a light and luscious sauce will cost you under 300 calories!

In this book you will find some classic names for sauces whose ingredients or methods may occasionally sound unorthodox. That's because my chief criterion has been *your* desire to lose weight.

Therefore, some of the recipes have been recast from their original form to make them less fattening. In the Pasta Diet, the emphasis is always on lowfat, low-calorie, low-cholesterol, natural dishes, with the accent on sound nutrition. That means that ample provision has been made in the dishes and recipes in this book to give you all the fiber, vitamins, and minerals you need in the tastiest way imaginable—via the garnishings and sauces accompanying your pasta.

Apart from seeing to it that you lose weight, one of my main objectives is to dispel the notion that Italian food is heavy and fattening. The sauces you will be creating are part of the *true* Italian cooking—light, flavorful, classic cooking—all under or about 300 calories a serving.

The heavy sauces common in American-style Italian cooking do only one thing: They camouflage the real tastes of food, in addition to being time consuming and unwholesome. You will find that a jar of "Italian seasoning," or some freshly ground black or white pepper will do more to accent the vegetables than any heavy oil-based dressing. With the methods set forth in the Pasta Diet you will bring out the real flavor and tastes of food. Butter, flour, and cream are "texturizers"; they add a certain consistency to a dish but basically they do not add much flavor. A quarter of a cup of dry wine, herbs, and spices can add as much taste and texture as any amount of butter or cream and more!

To be exciting and satisfying, food should have a definite taste: It should be hot, sweet, tart, delicate, whatever. There's no question in my mind that the chief reason many people put on weight is *dull meals!*

Uninspired, run-of-the-mill, dull foods lead to a feeling of dissatisfaction, which leads to overeating. When you eat an exciting dish, you can be happy, and satisfied, with a small amount of food. One of the things you will learn on the Pasta Diet is to stress quality over quantity.

After following the Pasta Diet, your new figure will be the clearest proof of the success of your new Italian eating habits. You won't ever again think of pasta as only spaghetti with meatballs, fettucine Alfredo, or macaroni with cheese. And you will have banished utterly from your thoughts the idea of thick red sauce (Ugh!), heavy with meat and oil (Ugh!). Instead, you will pamper your palate and regale your family and guests with the zestful flavors of herbs, spices, and other seasonings. They are what I call "taste accenters," and they enhance flavor without adding weight.

You will cook without salt and without sugar, or butter, using only pure ingredients, fresh vegetables, and wine or fruit for sweeteners. You will make luscious cream sauces with nothing more than a cup of part skim ricotta, some Romano cheese, Italian seasoning, or fresh parsley.

This book offers hundreds of such sauces, each one a *de*calorized delight. Moreover, it will point the way to your creating your own versions of these sauces, a practice limited only by your own inventiveness.

PASTA ECONOMY AND PASTA PSYCHOLOGY

Pasta is a lowfat food (1.5 percent) and a valuable source of protein (15 percent). It contains eight of the essential amino acids (the pasta sauce generally provides the other amino acids), along with vitamins, minerals, and complex carbohydrates galore.

Pasta is versatile, easy to cook, and nutritious and it requires only a minimum of kitchen know-how. It allows you to glory in a scrumptious Linguine with Egg and Basil Sauce at a cost of only 272 calories, or in a Primavera Sauce made with zucchini, tomatoes, broccoli flowerets, herbs, and wine—for even fewer calories per serving. All these are unquestionable advantages that make pasta the diet food *par excellence*. But we have not yet exhausted pasta's amazing qualities!

The volume of pasta sales in the United States is now measured in hundreds of tons per year. It's as well distributed as table salt, being sold everywhere from the smallest corner grocery store to the biggest supermarket chains. The reason for this, above and beyond the advantages already mentioned, is its price.

The average portion of pasta in this book costs approximately 60 cents, and about $1.30 a portion with the sauce. In our inflationary times that is simply incomparable! And with price-consciousness looming especially large in gatherings where food is served in volume, nothing can beat pasta as an inexpensive alternative to meat, fish, and poultry at parties and dinners.

Pasta has even become the cheap "chic" food to serve at such occasions. It's as good and proper at the most formal of meals as it is at informal garden or beach parties and picnics.

In the gourmet cooking classes I have conducted, I have found that no matter how sensible a diet is, if one element is lacking, the diet will be a flop and the weight reduction, at best, temporary. Yes, there's a "psychology" to food, a mental attitude inspired by the very sight, smell, and taste of the elements of the diet.

Imagine yourself entering a home where you are greeted by the heavenly aromas of oregano and Parmesan. Wouldn't it make your mouth water? Imagine a plate of substantial and filling food set before you, that has about it, with its shapes, colors, and garnishings, a festive air and an aesthetically pleasing appearance. At your place also would be a long-stemmed glass of white wine, calorically low for the elegance it adds. This whole meal might cost you no more than 350 calories, yet, when you finished eating, you would feel as if you had partaken of a formal, full-course dinner.

Another part of the "pasta psychology" is learning to relax during a meal. In your relaxed state, your metabolism works better and you burn food calories properly. "Eat-and-run" plays havoc with your digestion and will never lead to lasting, successful weight loss.

The final element of "pasta psychology" has to do with self-expression. I mentioned earlier that you could serve pasta every day of the year without duplicating a sauce. I will go further and say that, theoretically it is possible for you to go months without serving the same sauce twice. It all depends on your willingness to experiment.

Though undoubtedly you will have your favorites among the recipes, your progress in the pasta way-of-eating will enable you to experiment on your own with the natural ingredients you have been taught to use. Pasta will allow you to discover and create masterpieces of your own, and you will find that pasta is not just Italian! It's equally at home with Chinese vegetables or with feta cheese, shrimp, or raisins.

Cooking with pasta makes counting calories fun.

3

For Slimness, Health, and Enjoyment: The Why and How of Pasta

Pasta, it has already been seen, is a wonderful diet food. As a slow-release complex carbohydrate, it helps control blood sugar and insulin swings. This not only reduces hunger pains. Even more important is the fact that by helping to control fluctuations in these levels, pasta exercises a wholesome influence over the vital question of your health.

Among pasta's many commendable qualities is its nutritional value with regard to life expectancy. According to researchers, when insulin levels get too high, blood cholesterol may shoot up—a factor in the cause of heart disease. While this is one of America's chief health problems, cardiovascular disease, as one nutritionist has pointed out, has a lower incidence among the peoples of Southern Europe where, over the dinner table, pasta reigns supreme.

In Italy it is believed that, thanks to pasta, Italians enjoy a longer as well as a healthier life. In the country where pasta is king people live *twelve* years longer than Americans do.

That same idea is also at the heart of the Pasta Diet, the "balanced approach" as it is found in Italian cooking. It is a balance of all the right nutrients, with complex carbohydrates in sufficient quantities, along with vitamins, minerals and fiber, as well as protein and water. The sauce yields the needed fats (pasta itself is low in fats). And how surprising! Your calorie worries begin to melt away. Consuming fewer calories—as every dieter knows—is the first principle in getting slimmer. With neither carbohydrates nor protein numbering more than four calories per gram, you're well on your way with the Pasta Diet to achieving your goal.

It may even help you slim down while you're sleeping. It may even help you *sleep* better. The latter is because pasta is easier to digest, and as to the former—"slimming while you sleep" happens because the Pasta Diet is low in fats and "carbs." This combination allows calories to burn faster than they would in a combination including other or additional elements.

So on the Pasta Diet you lay aside the nagging anxiety over your calorie count. Your body itself will finally tell you what it needs. Given the right foods, your system loses the craving for additional helpings, thus reducing your calorie intake.

DID YOU KNOW . . .

that many diet foods have chemicals which "unbalance" your metabolism and that this often interferes with the process of losing weight?

I have noticed in myself, and in the attitudes of my friends, that food can actually make you "happy." It can give you that unmistakable feeling of contentment. However, the contrary is also true: some foods may make you angry or depressed, moody or irritable.

Is it possible that something you eat as part of your diet can make you . . . aggressive? Well, it most certainly can! Several reasons may account for the fact that some foods behave so shamefully, but one of them is more than likely to be that the dish in question simply does not supply enough calories.

The dieter recognizes this condition because it leaves behind a craving, one trouble you are spared with the Pasta Diet.

Can you be in good spirits if you are constantly hungry? I say, no, you can't be. Therefore, the "balanced carb" approach is ideal: by being "filling" it cuts down on the yen for food, that same "yen" which is the bane of all dieters.

VARIETY, VARIETY

Why do you think nature has provided us with seasonal foods? I like to believe it is because in nature itself is implanted the principle of variety, a principle that may be extended to all of nature's products but *especially* to pasta.

The variety to which pasta lends itself allows you to change your diet daily. This should include a wide range of fresh foods. An effective weight-loss program must incorporate variety—not always an easy task, but a cinch with pasta.

Because of its versatility, a diet based on at least one portion of pasta daily avoids the pitfall of most diets, that is, that eating grows routine and monotonous. Weight loss under such a regime becomes difficult because the sameness of the food weakens the will to persevere. Further, dull dieting also poses the question of food allergies, since increased exposure to an allergen in a particular food can develop into an intense allergic response if the routine remains unchanged.

In the Pasta Diet you'll find an eating program that has proved itself dramatically. People following it have not only dropped pounds, but have benefitted as well from being launched on a path of sound eating. The Pasta Diet, besides being delicious, is healthful. It keeps the level of energy high while keeping the swings of blood sugars down.

On the Pasta Diet, you can reach your desired weight-loss goal by mixing and matching any of the delicious menus in this book to suit your preferences and lifestyle. When your ideal weight has been reached you may add suggested variations.

To ensure weight loss, it is important to select the combinations and portions as recommended and use only the suggested products. It is also advised that you drink at least 4 to 6 glasses of water daily.

WATER: AN ESSENTIAL NUTRIENT

Every function of the body uses water. It is needed for digestion, absorption, circulation, excretion, transporting nutrients, helping to build tissue, and maintaining body temperature.

Through perspiration and other bodily functions a large amount of water is steadily being lost from the body each day. When the body consumes too much salt, it *retains more* water than it needs. This is the reason why many people retain fluid.

But more important for the diet, water also assists in diminishing the appetite. Researchers found that dieters who drank water liberally lost weight faster than those, following the same regimen, who did not drink as much (4-6 glasses a day).

COFFEE, MINERAL WATER, OR WINE?

It's my belief that many people become addicted to caffeine because their bodies are starved for true nourishment and crave something. The Pasta Diet, being "filling" and various, dispenses with the need to drink a large amount of coffee. This is all to the good because it is best to avoid drinking coffee while dieting.

Some people, knowing that coffee is harmful to proper digestion, use decaffeinated coffee. What they may not know, however, is that even decaffeinated coffee contains at least some of the active ingredient. Caffeine can play a nuisance role in dieting not only because it can make you "edgy." It also stimulates the blood sugars, first elevating them so that they plunge afterwards, with consequent havoc to your system.

A seesaw of this kind abets your hunger cravings when they are most dangerous—during meals. This is the time when the system being most vulnerable can least afford to be subjected to the effects of coffee, that is, when the blood sugar swings lead to overeating.

Rather than gulping coffee (at or away from the dinner table), if you must have coffee, cap off your meal with a cup of espresso. One cup after dinner makes up for all the cups of regular brew you normally take. Espresso has a more robust flavor because of the special roasting process which accentuates the taste.

Still, best of all, is to do without coffee entirely. Instead, have mineral water. It's good for digestion. You can choose from among many popular brands, the best being low in sodium as well. The Pasta Diet also allows herb teas, preferably those that do not have caffeine.

If you must snack on something more substantial than mineral water between meals, let it be fresh fruit or fresh vegetables. It's better to eat the whole fruit or vegetable than drink it in the concentrated form of juice. In addition, you get the benefit of the fiber, so essential for natural bowel function.

As for wine, the Pasta Diet allows two glasses (no more!) per day. And if you must have wine I prefer the dry Italian red and white varieties.

But if you can do without wine and/or coffee you can be sure that you will lose pounds more healthfully.

EATING OUT

As we all know, changing our fattening mode of eating means extending the change to all phases of our daily life.

The Pasta Diet is a permanent eating pattern, one that "travels" well and is easily adhered to in restaurants. Self-denial is not part of my program. Occasionally, you may order a dessert of cheesecake, as long as a few simple principles are maintained.

One of these principles has to do with salt. Tell the waiter that you do not want it in your order. The same goes for butter—tell him you like your entrees baked or broiled without it. Many restaurants will be pleased to prepare your order with olive oil or lemon juice instead.

When ordering pasta, ask for half portions. Try the fettucine, linguine, penne, or capellini (angel hair). Spinach or whole wheat noodles are fine. For the sauce, you'll always be safe with primavera (vegetable sauce), tomato and basil, pesto, fish, or ricotta.

Drink mineral water or dry wine only. Order fish, veal, chicken, or lamb. Avoid cream sauces and go very easy when sprinkling Parmesan cheese on top of the dishes you eat. Imported pastas are usually the rule in Italian restaurants deserving of the name. Because it is cheaper to make, homemade pasta, even in restaurants, is often prepared with all white flour! Do not order it!

DANGERS OF DRASTIC DIETS

The Pasta Diet is not a drastic regimen. It follows the principles of being effective, delicious, safe, and varied. With its emphasis on carbohydrates, it avoids the perils and pitfalls of other diets which may produce results in the very short run, but fail to maintain your weight loss—besides causing bodily harm.

High-protein/low-carbohydrate diets, for instance, deplete the body of water which accounts for the rapid weight loss. In such unwholesome diets, the loss of water (not fat) can lead to possible kidney damage. The scale, in this case, will show a water loss not a fat loss. A high percentage of the foods you eat should be in the form of complex carbohydrates and this has been incorporated into your Pasta Diet.

Drastic diets (less than 1200 calories a day) harm the body and do not result in a permanent weight (fat) loss. You need approximately 1200 calories if you're active.

It takes food (fuel) to make a fire (get your metabolism working). This is exactly what the Pasta Diet recommends: a lifestyle program based on wholesome foods and reasonable exercise.

4

It Is Easy to Be a Perfectionist in the Pasta Kitchen

To be fully effective and make good its promise of rapid weight loss, the Pasta Diet must be a total eating experience. This is no drastic innovation. The Italians, with their slim physiques and lively good health, have been eating this way for centuries. Like all great eating adventures, the Pasta Diet begins in the "kitchen."

Italians are known for their love of eating and drinking good wine. They love to create occasions for *festas* (celebrations.) But they also know how to respect the foods they eat. That's why the Pasta Diet is healthy, light, and exciting.

In the Pasta Diet, the ingredients are always fresh. The portions prepared, which are dedicated to the palate and health, are never large. You won't find the blockbusting "potato-protein connection" here. What you will find are light and tasty vegetables and salad instead. Little bread is eaten with the meal and instead of carbonated beverages or alcohol, there is wine or mineral water. Desserts and sugar products are not a regular part of the diet. Fresh fruit is the preferred dessert, though almond cakes and cookies are allowed from time to time, and ricotta cheesecake may make a delightful calorie-counted treat on other occasions.

NUTRITIONAL ENHANCERS

Pasta has finally been recognized as the nutritional powerhouse of foods and a great "food for energy." But not any type of pasta will give you the total nutritional benefits. *The quality durum wheat pastas* and popular vegetable and herb-based pastas mixed with quality durum wheat are highest in nutritional value. I have found that some American pastas, such as Prince macaroni, available in supermarkets, use 100% durum wheat. I was so impressed with the Prince Company's products that I agreed to serve as their official spokesperson.

The valuable properties of pasta are further augmented by the nutritional balance of properly cooked vegetables, fresh herbs, onions, garlic, and the right oil. Then there are, in addition, the proper portions of fish, chicken, veal, and lamb.

(The Pasta Diet does not recommend beef on a steady basis. It is high-fat heavy protein and hard to digest. Doing without beef, however, should be no hardship after your palate has become accustomed to the satisfying and exciting pasta recipes with fish, veal, chicken, and lamb. You will come to find beef heavy, and boring in taste.)

Some Other Nutritional Enhancers

- Tofu (ground soybeans of a smooth, white creamy texture) contains the highest levels of protein—superior to meat, as well as healthier and easier to digest. Use tofu in pasta sauces, salads, egg dishes, and as a topping instead of cheese.

- Alfalfa sprouts are highly nutritional and low in calories. Best raw, use them in sauces and salads.
- Wheat germ sprinkled over salads and in sauces is a high source of vitamins and iron.
- Oatmeal is not only a great protein food in the morning, but can also be used as a base for sauces for lunch or dinner. (My mother loves to put tomato sauce over oatmeal and sprinkle it with wheat germ or tofu—actually a perfect high-energy food that is low in calories, fat, and cholesterol.)

    Mix regular oatmeal (either plain oatmeal or the grain-type available in health food stores, *not* the quick-cooking variety) with fresh fruit, wheat germ, and tofu. Honey can be used as a sweetener . . . a powerful starter in the morning that will hold you all day.

- Ricotta should be used for cream sauces or for a cheesy taste. Better by far than regular cheese, which is loaded with salt, has a high-fat content, and is very high in calories. The same goes for cream. Ricotta is high in protein and low in calories. Get the much lighter, part skim variety.

BE A PERFECTIONIST

Italians are perfectionists, especially when it comes to cooking. Thus, a simple dish of Pasta al Olio can only be made perfect if the right ingredients are used.

This energy recipe, for instance, calls for oil, garlic, and hot pepper, but in order to ensure a result that pleases and excites, you must use the finest olive oil, crushed fresh garlic, and fresh dried hot peppers crushed very fine. The pasta should be cooked *al dente*, and the sauce must be timed.

The Pasta Diet was developed so that you can lose

weight quickly or maintain your weight at the desired level while eating sumptuously without sacrificing your health. The diet was approved and tested by six top nutritional experts and four doctors.

Adhering closely to the ingredients prescribed can make a remarkable difference in the way you look and feel. The herbs and spices that are part of the zesty recipes may even clear the body of harmful toxins. Fresh herbs and spices are not only the finest taste enhancers, but they help detoxify the body by acting as "cleansers" while aiding digestion.

Because toxins stop the body from functioning properly, they are detrimental to weight loss. Therefore, never use chemical products. You may, however, use canned imported Italian tomatoes (the plum variety) if fresh plum tomatoes cannot be found. The imported tomatoes have more taste, better texture, and fewer chemicals. (If you cannot find imported tomatoes in your area, Progresso makes an excellent plum tomato or crushed tomato sauce that can be found in supermarkets.) Canned tunafish, sardines, and clams are also acceptable when fresh products are unavailable.

HERBS

For centuries herbs have been used to enhance the flavor of food. Fresh herbs bring a definite taste to the dish while offering countless health benefits.

America is now discovering the humble herb. It is finally learning to employ the versatility of this marvelous ingredient. Home gardens are becoming popular, and markets and gourmet shops are beginning to sell a variety of fresh herbs.

The secret of Italian, and of many of the international cuisines, has been the use and balance of fresh herbs. It is, therefore, very important to know the proper herbs, how to use them, and how to grow or purchase them. You should also know what jarred herbs will work in a pinch and how to store them properly.

Here are some of the important herbs to use in the Pasta Diet.

- *Basil*—This is the most popular and widely used herb. Always use fresh. Whether large or small, leafed, diced, puréed, or chopped, basil adds a pungent taste to tomato sauces, wine sauces, and cheesy-garlicky pesto sauces.

    Buy fresh basil leaves as needed and store them in plastic bags in the refrigerator. Keep in mind that basil is delicate and will last only a few days. If you plan to keep it longer, put the leaves in a jar and cover them with oil to seal out the air. The leaves will stay fresh and green. Using this method, the basil can be stored for up to a year, as long as you keep the leaves under a layer of vegetable or olive oil. (Avoid freezing, as the leaves become dried and tasteless.)

    Basil should be added to a sauce at the last minute to impart the strongest taste.
- *Italian Parsley*—This wide, flat-leafed parsley has 90 percent more taste than the standard curly leafed parsley.

    Dice the leaves only and cook with the sauce, adding more at the last minute. Diced parsley can be stored in air-tight plastic containers and frozen.
- *Dill*—fresh dill and jarred dill weed (but preferably fresh). Dill is good with wine and lemon sauce, cream sauces and dressings, mustard sauces, or sprinkled over fish, eggs, tuna, potatoes, chicken, or veal. Use fresh dill immediately; it is very perishable and turns yellow and dry quickly. Dill weed in a jar can last for up to two months.
- *Tarragon*—Fresh tarragon is used with fish, chicken, or veal and in salads and with vegetables. Use fresh tarragon leaves, diced very fine. For the best flavor, do not cook but add at the last minute.
- *Fresh Mint*—Freshly ground mint leaves are used as a touch in pesto sauce (for a more creative and light

fresh taste) and, of course, in freshly made mint sauce for lamb, veal, or chicken.

- *Garlic*—Not only is the pungent garlic extremely healthful, but it is the key to more classic sauces than I have space to mention. However, let's simply begin with the proper use.

    Always use fresh garlic cloves. Peel and mash in a garlic press or with a knife. (This is the secret in preventing "garlic breath," because when garlic is crushed, it becomes a creamy paste with the juices disbursed evenly throughout the sauce. When you bite into a chunk of garlic, it breaks onto the roof of your mouth and causes garlic breath!)

- *Nutmeg*—Freshly grated nutmeg is used in many classic recipes to enhance the taste of spinach, ricotta, and eggplant. Use just a pinch for a great accent and taste enhancer.

- *Cayenne Pepper*—Always, always use cayenne pepper rather than black pepper in cooking. Not only is it more healthful and easier to digest, but it is superior in bringing a "piquant" taste to a sauce. In the final cooking process, add a pinch (not too much); keep tasting until you get the right "hot taste" you want.

- *Hot Red Pepper Flakes*—These come in jars and are used to make a hotter sauce base. Add them at the beginning of the cooking process when sautéing the onions, garlic, and other ingredients.

    Fresh, crushed red peppers provide a better tasting, fresher "hot accent."

- *Italian Seasoning*—This is a must! The perfect balance and mixture of spices, this blend gives just the right taste of oregano (most people add too much of this very overpowering herb), marjoram, rosemary, basil, sage, and thyme. In short, it is a perfect balance for use in many sauces, combined with fresh herbs.

Replace your jar of the Italian seasoning every two months, as jarred herbs dry quickly and lose taste and texture.

UTENSILS

Certain utensils are necessary for successfully preparing pasta dishes. I am sure most kitchens are equipped with three basic utensils. However, it's important to mention the "pasta basics" in order to ensure perfectly cooked pasta every time. Needless to say, the finest equipment will ensure the best results.

- *A large pot with a cover:* 8- to 10-quart size, copper, heavy aluminum, cast iron or porcelain coated. Pasta needs lots of rapidly boiling water to cook properly, as well as the room to "move" so it won't stick together. (A small pot filled with water will cause the pasta to stick and cook unevenly; pasta needs space to cook properly, no matter what the shape.)
- *Large colander:* To drain the pasta. The same type you would use for rinsing the vegetables and lettuce for a salad. The larger, the better, in order to catch the pasta and provide room for rinsing the pasta properly.
- *Large wooden forks:* To stir the pasta the minute after you add it to the rapidly boiling water. (Stir a few times through the cooking process, in order to keep the pasta from sticking.) Test the pasta by using the wooden fork to pull out a few strands to give them the *al dente* test (biting the pasta to see if it is firm enough, that is, not mushy).
- *Large pasta bowl:* To toss the pasta with cheese and sauce as well as to serve it in. Could be glass, decorated porcelain, or copper (which retains the heat and keeps the pasta warm), *but not plastic.* The large bowl can be held for a moment over the boiling water as the pasta is cooking in order to heat the bowl. (This will keep the pasta warm.)
- *Cheese grater:* There are many varieties on the market, from stainless steel to plastic. Always use fresh cheese that you grate at the last minute or at most a few hours before.

- *Large jar with a lid:* To store the fresh Parmesan, Romano, or Pecorino cheese that will be grated over the pasta at the last minute. Store the fresh chunks of cheese coated with olive oil in the jar in the refrigerator to ensure freshness. Be sure to punch holes in the top to allow air to flow through.

- *Garlic press:* This is a must to ensure the right consistency of creamy, crushed garlic in the sauce. Garlic crushers come in stainless steel, plastic, or cast iron. Look for the type with larger holes that is easy to use.

- *A large heavy frying pan:* Your best utensil for a good sauce, as sautéing is the process of cooking rapidly and quickly. A large cast-iron or copper pan is best for retaining the heat. But a heavy aluminum pan or one that is porcelain coated will also be fine. The new nonstick coated pans are quite good as long as the pan is heavy aluminum and the coating is thick.

- *A small frying pan:* Made of cast iron, copper, or heavy aluminum, this type of pan is good for sautéing a small quantity of food, or when you need to sauté an ingredient separately.

- *Medium-sized saucepan:* Made of heavy aluminum, cast iron, or copper, this type of pan is used for boiling or cooking down certain sauces. The heavier the pan, the better you'll be able to control the heat and cooking process.

- *Bowls:* Glass is best, but copper, steel, aluminum, or plastic can be used. Important for mixing ingredients. A variety of sizes is preferred—large, medium, and small.

- *Knives:* It's very important to have good cutting knives (a chef guards his knives carefully and even travels with them). They are necessary for properly cutting the ingredients and making the task easier and quicker.

    The best professional knives are made of carbon, but it's very difficult to keep them clean and sharp.

The new stainless steel knives work very well. A variety of sizes: 2 small knives, 1 medium-sized, and 1 large carving-type knife. (Keep the knives sharp with a knife sharpener.)

- *Wooden spoons:* Indispensable for stirring sauces and tasting. Have at least three different sizes of wooden spoons, including those with longer handles.
- *Individual pasta bowls:* The best type of dishes to serve pasta, both for the sauce and to keep the pasta warm, are medium-sized pasta bowls. There are some very colorful varieties, as well as elegant crystal or glass bowls.
- *Pasta measuring tube:* This is a fairly new invention that saves time and answers the question "How much pasta should I cook?" It is available for 2, 4, 6, or 8 people. Usually 3 to 4 ounces is the proper amount (depending on whether the pasta is the first course or main course; don't go over 4 1/2 ounces!).
- *Blender or Cuisinart:* For puréeing and blending sauces and herbs.

5

"Pastatechnica": The Art of Preparation for Home and Entertaining

The Pasta Diet is quick, economical, healthy, delicious, satisfying, and, last but not least, easy to prepare. Most diets are "restrictive" in some form or another, usually entailing a lot of fuss and bother. The Pasta Diet alone, built around the traditional Italian staple, makes losing or maintaining weight a cinch. And "Pastatechnica" makes it even easier.

"Pastatechnica" is my term for the shortcuts, time-savers, and helpful hints which cooking with pasta has taught me since the time I was knee high. Knowing these techniques, I've always commiserated with the American housewife to whom the kitchen is often a place of toil and trouble.

"Pastatechnica" is even more important for the dieter. Most diet books make the business of losing weight not just unhealthful or even dangerous, but they encumber their menus with complex and time-consuming cooking preparations. The Pasta Diet sees to it that you spend more time at the dinner table than in the kitchen.

TIME CONTROL

Time control in my book is not a matter of hours but of minutes. Just keep in mind a very simple "order of procedure." What requires the most time to prepare must be done first. The rest follows as naturally as putting one foot in front of the other. (I almost said "it's easy as pie"—but, of course, I meant "pasta.")

Here's the basic "Pastatechnica."

- Be sure to open the red wines before starting the cooking preparations; red wine needs to "breathe" for at least 15 minutes before serving. For white wines, serve slightly chilled (dry white wine prepares the palate and does not change the taste of food).
- Fill a large pot with cold water and cover the pot. Turn the heat to high to bring the water to a boil. (Oil is unnecessary unless you're using the very soft homemade pasta.) Salt is a matter of taste; it's not really needed to cook pasta, but if you must have it, add the salt after the water comes to a boil. (Salt will, of course, change the taste of the pasta.)
- While the water comes to a boil, use a large frying pan to start your sauce. Begin by pouring a small amount of oil into the frying pan, then either dice the ingredients right into the pan (using the quick-cooking method), or dice, chop, mince, and crush the necessary ingredients on a chopping board. Then add the ingredients that take longest to sauté; wait a few minutes and add the remaining ingredients. (Don't add one ingredient at a time!) The onions, garlic, mushrooms, vegetables, chicken, etc., are all sautéed together—the herbs are added last.
- You can speed up the process by undercooking the pasta, draining it, and adding it immediately to the cooked sauce. Toss thoroughly. Cook a few minutes before serving the pasta (to complete the cooking of the pasta) and again mix the sauce throughout. Add a pinch of freshly grated cheese and fresh herbs.

- With the sauce and pasta completed and placed on the back of the stove, prepare the second course, or the salad and the dessert. (Don't serve bread with the pasta.)

TIME-SAVERS

The Pasta Diet is the basic Italian way of eating modified to melt away pounds of body fat. But I've seen time and again what happens when a last-minute food preparation is necessary, and one or several pasta ingredients cannot be found in the cupboard. Most often, hasty—and fattening—substitution is invented on the spot and the careful calorie balance of the Pasta Diet goes out the window. Therefore, I recommend you keep your kitchen stocked with the necessary ingredients.

The Pasta Diet is so effective because its simplicity allows you to be prepared at all times, not just for more elaborate dinners, but as well for quick meals, snacks, or party food.

Here's a basic list of what to keep on hand for all eating occasions.

- A variety of pastas: Always the imported kind, vegetable pastas, durum, whole wheat in different colors, shapes, and sizes. Pasta can be stored for a long time on the shelf in unopened boxes or cellophane bags. (If opened, it's best kept in the refrigerator.)
- Onions, garlic, and a variety of plain frozen vegetables (no sauces). Plain cut frozen vegetables (broccoli, spinach, zucchini, or mixed vegetables) can be used in pasta sauces or to accompany fish, veal, and chicken—or to top pizza.
- Freshly grated Romano or Parmesan cheese (or keep chunks in the refrigerator and grate as the pasta is served). For cheesy sauces, keep containers of skim ricotta cheese in the refrigerator.

- Cans of tunafish and sardines (packed in water, soy, or vegetable oil, without salt); frozen chicken breasts, fish, or frozen entrées from the new "light cuisine" can be easily added to a sauce or served with pasta.
- Herbs and Spices. Pots of fresh basil, tarragon, etc. (You can put fresh basil leaves in a jar, cover them with oil, and store them in the refrigerator.) Keep Italian seasoning on hand in a jar, as well as hot red pepper flakes, cayenne pepper, and dill weed.
- Cans of imported plum tomatoes from Italy, or Progresso crushed tomatoes.
- Grey Poupon mustard—a "must."
- Leftovers. Great to add to pasta and to make pasta salads quickly.

THE TEN-MINUTE PASTA DIET MEAL

1. Start the water boiling.
2. Prepare the sauce and salad at same time.
3. Add precut vegetables to large frying pan with oil, onions, and garlic; cover and cook for 8 to 10 minutes.
4. Have an easy-to-serve type of dessert: almond cakes, cookies, or fresh fruit.

LOW-CALORIE COOKING WITH WINE

Cooking with wine is finally coming into its own in America. For a long time it's been the custom in Europe and especially in Italy, the largest producer of wine in the world.

The wonderful thing about cooking with wine is that the calories and the alcohol content are burned off in the cooking process while the taste remains. Use wine to enhance the taste of a recipe or to replace stock, cream, or water in a sauce.

It is important to use quality wine and I recommend Italian wines. With their abundance of grapes, Italians do not need to "stretch" their wine with chemicals. Nor do they need to add sugar: The climate and the soil take care of that.

If you can't buy Italian wines, buy private estate-bottled wines which are usually not so heavy in chemicals and sugar. (The large jugs of mass-produced wines are full of chemicals and additives, thus contributing an enormous amount of unnecessary calories to the wine.) Most low-calorie wines on the store shelves are among the purest and best wines.

By the way, I serve my guests the same wines I cook with—after all, I don't use more than 1/2 to 1 cup of wine for cooking—because it does affect the taste of the sauce. Quality ingredients ensure quality in taste.

Here are some further wine tips:

- Add red wine to a pasta sauce before adding the tomatoes, or just use the wine as the cooked-down sauce base.
- Use white wine with chicken or veal with herbs and lemon.
- Use semisweet Marsala with veal or desserts.
- Use champagne in pasta sauces, ricotta sauces, and desserts.

ITALIAN WINES. . .

go for $3 and up; good whites from $4.50; reds from $5.

ENTERTAINING

I know people who refuse dinner engagements because they do not want to face a bombardment of heavy, fattening, and unwholesome dishes. But they never turn down my invitations. They know that I live by the Pasta Diet and that what's awaiting them at my home is a delicious and exciting meal with a minimum of calories.

(Sometimes I don't tell them until after dinner that they've been feasting on low-calorie food, and I really enjoy their expressions of disbelief.)

I am not at all surprised that pasta has become the "in" food for entertaining. No food lends itself better to a quick, economical, and festive array than the great variety of pasta colors and shapes. The "short" shapes—ziti, shells, elbows, swirls, wheels, or bows—look marvelously playful. And then the colors—spinach, tomato, and wheat-colored pasta: green, red, and golden—what a joy to the eye!

Sauces for the pasta vary according to the occasion, your own taste, and that of the guests. In this book you will learn how easy it is to choose any of several low-calorie sauces, whether they be vegetable sauces, seafood sauces, ricotta-based sauces, or all the other combinations set forth in the menu plans or suggested by your own imagination.

There are innumerable sauces to choose from, but among those excellent for every occasion are:

- The Primavera (mixed diced vegetables) or mixed seafood (for example, clams, shrimp, calamari, crab, scallops, lobster, diced white fish). Use sauce of tomato and herbs or vinaigrette herbs, decorate with olives and pimientos.
- Pesto sauce (either plain or with a touch of mint). Or a sauce of pesto with diced chicken and short pasta shapes (for example, green shapes with a sauce of ricotta cheese, mushrooms and diced tomatoes, using an oil, herb, or vinaigrette dressing).
- Eggplant sauces are very good for buffets. You can use short-shaped pasta with diced eggplant and tomato

sauce. Or Eggplant, Olives, and Zucchini Sauce with pasta and Chicken Sarna. Or short green pasta with diced chicken in a sauce of capers, white wine, mustard, olives, and lots of fresh chopped dill—served hot or at room temperature.

As the menu section will show you, the variety of sauces is inexhaustible, and what's more, they're all delicious, festive, filling, and . . . *low calorie!*

THE LARGE DINNER PARTY OR BUFFET

The Pasta Diet enables you to entertain for a large group with ease and comfort and the assurance of rousing success. The sample "entertaining" recipes in this book will give you excellent ideas which need merely to be enlarged to the proper scale to fit the size of your party.

At this point, let me suggest a skeleton outline of how you may organize a buffet that keeps the spirit up while keeping the weight down:

Use two large pots to prepare the pasta and a large pot for the sauce. Precook the pasta (undercook it by 2 to 3 minutes), drain, rinse in cold water, and drain again. Then add some of the sauce. When you are ready to serve, heat the pasta and cook for another few minutes. Toss with more sauce and freshly grated cheese. A pasta salad can be made the morning before the party or a few hours before serving.

THE "SEGRETTO" METHOD

This is a great time-saver as well as a "pasta saver."
It facilitates the proper timing for serving the pasta. You
can prepare the sauce and the pasta in advance and
heat them both (stirring the sauce to prevent sticking)
just before serving.

(Don't forget: When you prepare the pasta, undercook it so that it requires another 2 to 3 minutes of cooking time. Drain, then rinse the pasta in cold water to stop
the cooking process.) Add the pasta to the sauce and
toss through.

If you are not going to serve the pasta within an hour,
you can put the pan in the refrigerator. Take it out about half
an hour before serving and heat it for 2 to 5 minutes before
putting it on the table. Pasta can be frozen in glass bowls
using the "Segretto" method. With the Pasta Diet, you are
always ready to entertain by being able to prepare a great
pasta dish, sauce and all, within minutes.

Additional freshly grated cheese and additional sauce
should be passed at the table when serving the pasta. Also,
have a pepper mill available for adding freshly ground
pepper. If the sauce contains fresh basil, a small bowl of
chopped fresh basil should be placed on the table for
serving.

The salad and mixed fruit dessert can be made in
advance. (It's the chopping that's time consuming; the rest
can be managed very quickly.) For a real treat, take your
diced fruit salad and toss it with some liqueur, such as
Kirsch, Framboise, Cointreau, or Amaretto. (If you heat it for
a few minutes before serving, you will burn off the sugar
calories and alcohol content.) Another excellent dessert,
which is well in line with the Pasta Diet, may consist of a
pretty tray of almond cookies, fresh fruit, fruit tart, or ricotta
cheesecake, served with espresso.

It's important to keep the portions small; three to four
small portioned courses are much more exciting and

satisfying than a table groaning with one or two "heavy" dishes. If serving two to three courses, use approximately 3 to 4 ounces of pasta per course, and 4 ounces of either chicken, fish, or veal, along with the vegetables or salad. (Always use oil, not butter; use a lemon or vinegar dressing with safflower oil, vegetable, or preferably green extra virgin olive oil for the salad.)

SERVING IDEAS

Pasta is the party food par excellence for a reason that has nothing to do with its chief advantages of economy, ease of preparation, deliciousness, wholesomeness, and slimming properties. Over and beyond all these, the pasta courses are a visual delight that enhance the party atmosphere. You will find that the buffet, resplendent with tastefully presented food and pleasing decorations, is sure to delight your guests while making "entertaining" easy and enjoyable for the host or hostess.

Because of my show business background, I probably do more than most people to "stage" my sit-down dinner parties. I tend to approach such occasions much like a theatrical production in which my pasta menu has the leading role.

I make my place settings attractive with color-coordinated napkins and a small vase with a flower at each plate. I further create a festive impression with flowers and candles. I find that this emphasis on visual presentation is half the pleasure of dining (as the better-class restaurants have long known). The appeal to the eye is curiously satisfying to the stomach. You'd be surprised to discover how losing weight is facilitated by paying attention to the visual details of the dining experience.

Buffets, in particular, should be planned to appeal to the eye. The menus from the Pasta Diet lend themselves most gracefully to an exciting blending of color, texture, and taste. In the case of the sauce, for instance, match the color of the sauce to the shape and color of the pasta. Green noodles look attractive with a red (tomato) sauce, or use a creamy white ricotta sauce over green fettucine or spaghetti. The white or wheat-colored pastas especially need colorful sauces, such as Primavera (mixed vegetables), tomato, seafood, mushroom, or eggplant.

To serve the pasta, use small glass or decorated bowls, soup dishes, or large warmed plates (if it's a main-course dish). Serving *casa lingua* or "family style" from a large bowl at the table is the way it is done in Italian homes on informal occasions. Plan to have either all dry white wine, or red, or start with a dry white and serve a red wine with heavier courses (veal, chicken, beef).

Remember that the short-shaped pasta is ideal for buffets. Buffet food should always consist of small bite-sized pieces of food because they are easier to serve and balance on one's lap. For entertaining large groups there is no better combination than short-shaped pasta with an exciting sauce and diced chicken, fish, veal, and beef, with chopped salads.

"POSH" PASTAS

To make plain pastas "posh" requires a little extra flair but not much in extra cost.

Here are some examples of the "posh" pastas you can safely consume without jeopardizing your weight-loss program.

Rolled green lasagne noodles stuffed with luscious fillings, such as

- Salmon, with mustard and dill sauce, covered with pesto sauce; vegetable timballo (layers of pasta noodles and vegetables served in wedges like a pie covered with ricotta sauce); or three kinds of pasta on one dish (separate small portions with different tastes; for example, green noodles with red sauce, red with pesto sauce, and white with vegetable sauce)

- Fettucine noodles with caviar, vodka, and a touch of cream
- Seafood sauce over green noodles served in a huge seashell
- Mixed, three-color pasta with vegetable purées
- White fettucine noodles with pieces of salmon, peas, and zucchini
- Corkscrew pasta with scallops and broccoli sauce (also served as a pasta salad)
- Tagliarini Verde alla Bruno (fettucine with tomatoes, goat cheese, and mushrooms)
- Pasta, string beans, and almonds (pasta salad)
- Macaroni Vegetable Stew
- Codfish and Pasta Stew
- Tuna and Pasta Chowder
- Stuffed pasta shells with meat, vegetables, seafood, or ricotta
- Roasted Chicken with Pasta Salad
- Chicken Tarragon Pasta Salad
- Spaghetti Primavera with Pesto Sauce
- Spinach Gnocchi with Tomato-Basil Sauce
- Spinach and Ricotta Gnocchi with Pesto Sauce
- Seafood Primavera with Swirl Pasta

6

Pasta with Vegetables

Vegetables and pasta originated in my birthplace, the hills of Abruzzi, and is a dish common in all the regions of Italy. This old Italian peasant recipe has become a "chic" item on American menus as "Pasta Primavera," and I should be guilty of false modesty were I not to claim my share in raising it to this august position—I gave it the name "Primavera."

I started writing articles and advising restaurants on the marvelous qualities of the simple combination of pasta and vegetables about a dozen years ago. I have demonstrated this dish on some 150 talk shows all over the country, and on many a day, at 6:30 in the morning, with sleep still in my eyes, I whipped up the "Primavera" on an early morning television program, "The Today Show." I knew that success was assured when even at that ungodly hour the crew, director, and host dug in unabashedly.

They were astonished that a meal could be so light and yet so satisfying. And they were entranced by the "figures"—a mere 425 calories for a 3-1/2-ounce portion. Those who were vegetarians rejoiced at the Primavera's perfect balance of protein and vegetables.

In my own Pasta Diet, the Primavera ranks tops not just for its obvious advantages to the weight-losing or weight-watching person. Primavera can be served as an appetizer, main course, or side dish without the pasta. Your own inventiveness in combining vegetables is the limit to the Primavera's astonishing variety.

In Italy, depending on the availability of the vegetables, as well as the particular region, fresh vegetables of the season are used. These vegetables are usually zucchini, eggplant, broccoli, mushrooms, asparagus, and tomatoes. Often one vegetable is used to make the pasta sauce base.

I recommend that you stick closely to these traditional Italian "Primavera" vegetables that I recommend. I've seen chefs add their own personal touch of creativity with snow peas, carrots, celery, peas, corn, string beans, etc. wrong! No added taste—wrong texture. On top of this, I've seen them use butter and cream! When I tasted such abortions, I made silent apology to my forebears in the mountains of Abruzzi for the sacrilege being committed upon their sturdy peasant dish—and my creation for the Pasta Diet.

Primavera means springtime, the time when new vegetables begin to sprout. You will do honor to the name, while giving a treat to your palate, if you use the finest quality and freshest vegetables of the season. Be imaginative in your combinations for the sauce base. For instance, should you find fresh asparagus or baby eggplants in the market, join them with zucchini and either fresh Italian plum tomatoes or the canned imported type.

THE UNBEATABLE PRIMAVERA

Eat like a sturdy Italian peasant and Roman gourmet at the same time—and lose weight!

Simply sprinkle a small amount of oil into your frying pan, then add onions, crushed garlic, and fresh herbs. Add to these the diced vegetables. Cover and cook over low-to-medium heat for 5 to 8 minutes. Serve plain or add tomatoes and freshly grated cheese. You may favor a pinch of hot red pepper flakes or cayenne pepper for piquancy.

THE VERSATILE EGGPLANT

It took zucchini a long time to gain acceptance on American dinner tables. Now eggplant has come into its own. Though everyone knows about this marvelous vegetable, there is still confusion as to how to prepare it and what kind to buy.

Always buy the smaller eggplants, unless you are making baked eggplant slices or stuffed eggplant. Then you will need the larger size. Baby eggplants have more taste.

Eggplant is prepared in thousands of ways throughout every region in Italy. It is also very popular throughout the Middle East and Greece. But in Sicily it probably enjoys the greatest popularity.

When you walk into a Sicilian restaurant, you will see tables lined with as many as fifty versions of eggplant—just as appetizers! Then there are the eggplant variations featured on the menu, such as pasta with eggplant (forty versions), eggplant stuffed with pasta or fish, grilled eggplant with fresh herbs.

BASIC EGGPLANT

Be sure to soak the eggplant in salted water after dicing, slicing, or halving it. Cover the eggplant with cold water and salt and let it stand for 1/2 hour. Rinse and repeat again.

Small eggplants do not have the bitter taste of the larger ones, so they require less soaking—only about 10 minutes. Drain and spread out on paper towels or dry immediately. Then choose one of the many ways in which you can cook and serve this versatile vegetable.

As a very healthy, very low-calorie, and very practical food, eggplant can become a frequent part of your Pasta

Diet. Here are just a few of the many suggested ways to prepare it:

- Pasta à la Norma (eggplant slices grilled with tomato-herb sauce)
- Pasta with Eggplant Caponata (sautéed diced eggplant with olives)
- Peppers and Tomatoes with Fresh Herbs (and a dash of vinegar)
- Pasta with Eggplant and Zucchini
- Pasta with Eggplant and Ricotta Sauce
- Pasta with Puréed Eggplant Sauce
- Eggplant Stuffed with Pasta
- Eggplant-Ricotta Rolls
- Eggplant Lasagne
- Eggplant Parmesan
- Eggplant-Mushroom Sauce (served with pasta or risotto or chicken or veal)
- Baked and stuffed eggplant variations (meat, cheese, pasta, vegetables)
- Marinated Baby Eggplants
- Eggplant Caponata
- Puréed Eggplant Appetizer
- Eggplant-Ricotta Dip
- Grilled eggplant slices (as side dish)
- Eggplant Livornese Sauce
- Eggplant and Roasted Pepper Sauce
- Eggplant Primavera Sauce
- Eggplant Salad
- Eggplant and Pesto Sauce
- Eggplant Piccante Sauce (a hot sauce)

THE WONDERS OF ZUCCHINI

Zucchini has already secured an honorable place for itself in the American kitchen. Though it is popular in many menu items, especially salads, to my mind the zucchini is really at home only when it is cooked in the Italian manner.

For the person who wants to lose weight, the best thing about zucchini is that it is very low in calories yet very wholesome. But on any score, zucchini's delicate taste, texture, and versatility make it, for me, the perfect vegetable.

Zucchini is absolutely delicious in many pasta sauces as well as stuffed with pasta, fish, meat, or vegetables.

Zucchini can be sautéed with a great many different herbs, spices, vegetables, and meats. It is also delicate enough to be served with fish, veal, or chicken.

The smaller zucchini have more taste. (Italians always select smaller vegetables for that reason.) Use large zucchini only for stuffing or quantity. If you scrub the skins thoroughly, you can use the unscraped zucchini to add a colorful touch to a dish. Zucchini rings can be added to salads or served raw as appetizers with dips.

Here are just a few of the many ways in which this wonderful vegetable can be prepared.

- Use zucchini grated on top of salads or pastas (one of my little inventions!) Instead of grated cheese, use grated zucchini.
- Pasta Sauce with Zucchini and Mushrooms
- Zucchini and broccoli misto
- Zucchini and Potatoes (diced and sautéed with herbs and onions)
- Zucchini Lasagne
- Zucchini Pancakes
- Zucchini cake and cookies
- Zucchini ice cream

THE HUMBLE POTATO

The most underrated and undeservedly scorned item on a weight-reduction diet is the potato. In America, potatoes have earned the reputation of being fattening because we have suffered a fried potato boom. Anything fried in heavy oil is "fattening." But boiled, baked, or sautéed potatoes are not at all fattening. On the contrary, they are satisfying and nutritious and they won't add an ounce to your body weight.

I call potatoes a wonder food for their high levels of potassium (important to women) and their wealth of vitamins and minerals. You may safely vary your diet with potatoes and continue to slim down.

Just look at some of the simple and exciting ways to prepare the lowly tuber. (Note: Red-skinned potatoes are best.)

- Scrub potatoes and dice them; sauté with other vegetables or with leftover meat, chicken, or lamb; add onions, garlic, and herbs.
- Boil and slice potatoes (and use as a salad, with a dressing of oil, vinegar, and fresh herbs).
- Serve with tomatoes, eggs, tuna, or sardines.
- Serve with pesto sauce.
- Combine with zucchini, peppers, and mushrooms and sauté with herbs.
- Serve in marinara sauce.
- Baked potato skins stuffed with diced vegetables, fish, chicken, veal, or ricotta.

BAKED OR SWEET

For baked potatoes, use Idaho potatoes.

Scrub and bake in the skins. (Many of the nutrients are in the skins.) Bake at 350 degrees and serve with fresh chives and a dash of sweet (unsalted) butter, or mix the herbs with ricotta and use as a topping for the potatoes.

Bake and mash the potatoes, adding an oil, vinegar, and herb dressing.

For sweet potatoes, slash and bake as you do white potatoes; serve plain or mashed and puréed.

DON'T FORGET THE BLENDER

I consider the blender a blessing. Not only does it allow me to create a beautiful combination of puréed fruit desserts and sorbets in minutes, but it lends ease and joy to preparing a delicious pesto sauce, a puréed Primavera, or a luscious, creamy ricotta sauce, etc.

Here are some pointers about using this handy appliance for your Pasta Diet:

- Be sure the top bowl is clean and dry before starting.
- Remember that it is important to cut all the ingredients very small. Stop the machine often and stir the ingredients with a wooden spoon. (Caution: Don't stir while the machine is running.)
- Be careful not to overpurify or blend to the point of liquefying; run the machine for only a few seconds, then stir and taste the sauce. Continue until you have the right consistency.
- I highly recommend the new food processor machines for time-saving in chopping, dicing, shredding, mashing, and puréeing.

AND FOR THE PICNIC

Pasta variations are perfect for those times when you want to get away from it all. The hearty appetites worked up by hiking and swimming are marvelously satisfied with pasta salads that are delicious, low in calories, easy to serve, and very light, both to carry and to digest.

One of my picnic favorites from the Pasta Diet is a julienne of mixed vegetables over small shapes of pasta. Store in an air-tight plastic container. Always use a small amount of dressing, made with sesame, vegetable, or green extra virgin olive oil and red wine vinegar. Toss and add fresh herbs. Toss again before serving.

Also for that outing *al fresco* try . . .

• Puréed eggplant with small pita bread cubes to dip into the eggplant purée.
• Zucchini and chicken misto (cubed chicken lightly sautéed and mixed with diced zucchini and pimientos and tossed with a light herb dressing).
• Variety of pasta salads with: short shapes and sauces of vegetables, fish, chicken, veal, or pesto (vary colors and shapes).
• Vegetable lasagne (layers of eggplant spread with a thin sauce of vegetables and mushrooms).
• A raw vegetable platter of julienned carrots, celery, peppers, and zucchini served with a dip of ricotta and mustard with a pinch of curry powder or puréed eggplant or hot tomato sauce.
• Purée vegetables and use over brown bread cut into little squares. (Be sure to add enough herbs, onions, and ginger to make it tasty.)
• Marinated vegetables in oil and vinegar and herbs, used as a side dish.
• Eggplant pizzas. Grill eggplant rounds and top them with tomatoes and herbs or puréed vegetables or ricotta.
• Chicken in mustard and dill sauce.

FRYING WITHOUT OIL

Most new cookware has a coating that enables the cook to sauté without oil or with only a small amount of oil. Buy the better quality pans which have a thicker coating. (Coating that comes off the pan and mixes with the food could be dangerous.)

Select heavy cast-iron or copper pans. The weight assures even heat distribution. Thin aluminium pans do not heat evenly and can cause food to burn.

When you sauté shallots, the creamy, juicy sauce that is released makes a good base for sautéing—and little oil is needed.

You can also add 1 to 2 tablespoons of sesame, vegetable, or olive oil to the pan, twirl the pan, and pour the oil out, leaving only a thin coating in the pan.

7

Pasta with Seafood

As a child, I spent a lot of time in Pescara, one of Italy's most beautiful coastal resort towns. Two hours northeast of Rome, it is surrounded by an enormous mountain range and beautiful Adriatic beaches.

Pescara also happens to be the place where the finest seafood and pasta in Italy come from. The famous classical Italian Zuppa di Pesce (a soup of mixed seafood) originated in Pescara.

In this lovely coastal town, I enjoyed some of the most delicious seafood in the world. As a child, I was already acquainted with a wonderful diet which included mostly seafood, pasta, fresh vegetables, chicken, veal, lamb, fruits, and Italian white and red wine (which my father made), and I firmly believe that my childhood diet has had a beneficial effect on my life as an adult. I am happy to say that I've always had very good health and lots of energy. I look ten years younger than I am. (My husband says "fifteen years younger"—how kind!) I follow the same Pasta Diet I learned to eat as a child and I weigh as little as I did at sixteen.

SEAFOOD IS TOPS

Seafood is the perfect diet and health food. It is so light and can be prepared in so many ways.

Of course, when I talk about seafood, I'm not referring to the odious examples of fried fish. Those dried out, tasteless strips of cardboard-like substances dipped in tartar sauce or ketchup play havoc with both calories and digestion.

Many Americans are fortunate in that they can avail themselves of a wonderful variety of fresh seafood from both coasts. Others in the inland regions must usually rely on fresh-frozen seafood, but in either case for a healthful, slimming Pasta Diet, you can't go wrong when you choose fish or seafood.

Fresh fish is not only delicious but it has as much protein as most meats, weight for weight. It is low in calories and low in the saturated fatty acids that lead to an increase in serum cholesterol. Only a few fish are fatty, and even this depends on the season and the life cycle of the fish.

Supermarkets feature a great variety of fresh-frozen fish and more and more specialty fish markets are opening with an excellent choice of available fresh fish. Even though recent increased demand and a decrease in supply has made fish more expensive, I believe it is well worth the extra money not to deny yourself the best and freshest fish.

Of the many types of seafood that are low in calories and go well with the Pasta Diet, choose from among . . .

- White fish: fillet of sole, striped bass, flounder, red snapper, halibut, swordfish, cod, monkfish, salmon, tuna, and sardines.
- Shellfish: clams, lobster, mussels, calamari, scallops, oysters, shrimp, and crab.
- "Monk" lobster: Monkfish has become a less expensive substitute for lobster. A firm white fish, it can also be prepared in several ways: baked with

tomato or lemon, wine, and herb sauce or pesto, or mushroom-tomato sauce.

GRILLING

Grilling seafood and fish is an excellent idea; it tastes good and is low in calories. The grilling process requires only a drop of oil and allows the full flavor of the seafood and fish to be preserved. Either a professional grill on the stove or a barbecue grill works very well.

If you use a barbecue grill, put the seafood or fish on a sheet of aluminum foil or in small aluminum baking pans. Brush the fish with oil and sprinkle on fresh herbs and lemon juice. Be careful that the fire or grill is not too hot. Cook the fish just past the point of being raw (don't overcook it or the fish will become tough and tasteless). Be careful as to both the timing and the temperature. Delicate fish should be wrapped tightly in the foil. Firmer types, such as swordfish or striped bass, need no covering.

After removing the grilled fish, put it on warmed plates and pour more sauce over the fish (oil, lemon juice, and fresh herbs, such as parsley, tarragon, and some basil). Use the premixed Italian seasoning in a jar if you cannot find fresh herbs.

This is truly the classic way to serve fish anywhere in Italy. And as Italians believe in enjoying the taste of the fish rather than the coating, you'll be delighted that the recipes in the Pasta Diet allow the full flavors of the fish to come through, enhanced, not overwhelmed, by the sauce.

POACHING

This method is very popular because it ensures the lightness of the fish while maintaining a very low-calorie level (provided you don't pour a heavy sauce over the fish, as the French do!).

Use a fish poacher for fish of a larger size. For poaching a smaller fish, you can use a baking pan: Lay the fish on the bottom and cover with water, wine, or fish stock and fresh herbs, cover, and cook until the fish flakes when touched with a fork.

For an example of what you can do with pasta and seafood, take a look at the following sample of wonderful, delicious, and totally satisfying combinations:

- Baked Fish with Almonds
- Pasta with Clams (white and red)
- Stuffed Eggplant with Shrimp
- Macaroni Seafood Misto
- Shrimp in Garlic Sauce
- Sole Stuffed with Spinach
- Seafood Pasta Salad
- Seafood and Pesto with Pasta
- Seafood Primavera Sauce
- Fish Soup Abruzzi Style
- Calamari in Tomato Sauce

8

Pasta with Poultry and Meats

The average American diet is very high in protein (steaks, butter, and cheese) and very low in carbohydrates and fiber. The danger of this type of regimen is exemplified by the frightening statistics concerning cardiovascular diseases. The Pasta Diet reverses this trend, because it is high in complex carbohydrates and fiber and adequate in protein. Every doctor and nutritionist will confirm both the wholesomeness of the Pasta Diet and its effectiveness as a safe and proven weight-loss program.

Just because the Pasta Diet does not include a lot of beef and some other meats does not mean that they are to be eliminated from your Italian-style weight-loss program. If you follow the recipes, you will have your beef in some very delicious pasta combinations, but you won't overdose on it. For meats, the Pasta Diet favors chicken and veal.

In the menus you will find some of the most celebrated chicken and pasta dishes of the Italian kitchen. After fish, chicken is the preferred main-course food. The variety of chicken combinations is enormous, and the dishes are quick and easy to prepare.

You may, if you wish, substitute turkey for chicken.

Both are low in calories and simple to prepare. Chicken and turkey breasts are best because of their low-calorie content.

Skinless and boneless chicken or turkey breasts can be prepared, believe it or not, 250 different ways. Here are a handful of the most popular:

- Chicken with mustard, capers, and dill sauce
- Chicken and Eggplant Combination
- Chicken with Mushrooms and Wine
- Stir-Fry Chicken Italian Style
- Pasta and Chicken Salad
- Pasta and Chicken Pesto
- Chicken Primavera
- Linguine with Chicken Sauce

VEAL, THE PREFERRED DIET MEAT

I call veal "elegant." Thin and delicate, light and easy to digest, veal is unlike any other meat. High in protein and low in calories, it is almost not a meat at all!

In Italy, where the national taste embraces lightness and delicacy, veal is the preferred meat. Except in the Florence area, beef is very seldom served. Americans, too, have discovered that in taste and texture, veal is much more exciting than beef.

Veal is great alone, but with pasta, it's superb. It is elegant for entertaining and perfect for dieting since it makes light but exciting meals. It has only one drawback: It costs a little more than other meats, but I believe you'll find the extra expense well worth it. After all, delicious dining makes dieting painless, and that's the principle of the Pasta Diet.

Veal scaloppine (thinly sliced veal from the leg) is the most expensive; veal stew meat is the least costly. Don't forget that veal is very thin and delicate and must be cooked carefully—just a few minutes for the scaloppine. Veal stew meat can be used for sautéing with the sauces for pasta.

(And, by the way, you can substitute veal in all the dishes using chicken.)

Here is a foretaste of some of the veal delights in store for you on the Pasta Diet:

- Veal Limone Mancini
- Veal Marsala with Mushrooms
- Veal Piccata
- Veal Herbs alla Grille
- Veal, Mushrooms, Red wine sauce
- Veal, Eggplant, Tomato sauce
- Veal alla Creamy cheese sauce
- Veal Chops Sala
- Veal, Capers, and lemon sauce
- A Pasta Misto with diced veal, diced shrimp, and asparagus or diced veal with avocados and tomatoes.
- All great pasta sauces—perfect for leftover veal or inexpensive veal stew meat (sauté lightly with wine and herbs)

MAKING MEAT GO A LONG WAY

Using meat and leftovers with pasta is a great way to add a high-protein count to pasta and make it a one-dish meal. At the same time, it disposes of your leftovers in a tasty and satisfying fashion.

How to use ground beef other than hamburger? Sauté ground beef with onions, garlic, and herbs, add a dash of dry red wine, and serve over pasta (or add tomatoes and cook down).

Leftover steak or chops can be diced, sautéed with onions, herbs, and spices, a dash of wine, and behold!—a great low-calorie salsa!

Italy's most famous meat sauce is from a region called Bologna. Here's how you, too, can make this simple dish that's just delicious: pasta with meat sauce.

SALSA BOLOGNESE
(Meat Sauce with Wine and Tomatoes)

   1 tablespoon vegetable oil
   1 garlic clove, crushed
   1/4 cup chopped onion
   1/2 pound ground lean beef
   1/4 cup shredded carrots
   1/4 teaspoon Italian seasoning
   1/2 cup dry red wine
   2 cups drained canned imported Italian plum tomatoes
   1/4 cup chopped fresh parsley leaves

   1. Sauté the onion and garlic in the oil for 1 to 2 minutes. Add the ground beef, carrots, and herb seasoning. Mix well. Cook for 5 minutes and add the wine. Cook for 3 to 4 minutes.
   2. Add the tomatoes and cook for 8 to 10 minutes.
   3. Sprinkle the parsley over the sauce at the last minute. Serve with pasta, sprinkled with Parmesan cheese.

Variation
Add mushrooms or diced mixed vegetables. Sauté in the beginning with onions and garlic.

Time: 25 minutes
Servings: 6
Calories: 380 per serving

9

Pasta Salads

America is going through a pasta salad craze. Every little deli, supermarket, specialty shop—there are even more and more pasta shops—features a variety of pasta salads.

You can make these pasta salads a mainstay of your meals. They are easy to eat gracefully because they use the short shapes of pasta. They're simple to prepare and to keep on hand. You can change the pasta salad every day by adding various leftovers. The variety is endless. I have personally collected well over 500 versions.

BASIC PASTA SALAD
(The "All-in-One Meal")

Use a variety of short-shaped pastas and mix the shapes and colors. Use imported pasta shapes (ziti, shells, elbows, wheels, swirls, bows, and gnocchi shapes in green, white, and red).

Cook the pasta *al dente* (with a "bite") and cool it under cold water. Drain the pasta well and transfer it to a large bowl. Toss with 2 to 3 tablespoons of olive or safflower oil (so the pasta won't stick and the sauce will adhere to the pasta). Dice the various ingredients into the bowl and toss through the pasta.

Refrigerate the salad if you are not using it immediately. Pasta salads can be made a day ahead of time.

ALWAYS IN STYLE

Pasta salad is popular because it's ideally suited to today's lifestyle, easy to prepare, carry, eat, and serve. It's light, an unsurpassed diet food, exciting, satisfying . . . and always "in style."

On one occasion, I invited the cast of a movie I worked in to come to my house after a rehearsal. Richard Chamberlain, Faye Dunaway, James Garner, and twelve others came. I served them some wine and started boiling the water and dicing ingredients to make the sauce for a huge pasta salad. That night I combined leftover diced chicken, with tomatoes, pimientos, peppers, and zucchini. I sprinkled some olives on top, and then tossed it with oil, vinegar, and herbs.

Well, the cast was amazed at how quickly and easily I'd conjured up the delicious treat. And when I revealed that the calorie count was no more than 250 calories per 3-ounce portion, they were astounded.

A pasta salad allows you to take it easy. It enables you to be creative by using whatever food you have on hand: vegetables, seafood, leftovers, or anything else that is available. Pasta salad lends itself to every setting, from a romantic interlude on the beach with a good bottle of wine and fresh fruit to the "all-in-one" low-calorie dinner table, the festive buffet, a party, picnic, or family lunch or supper.

Keep pasta salads mixed in your refrigerator. They're even great in the morning (add eggs and cheese).

Always keep boxes of imported pasta on hand in a variety of shapes and colors, and you'll be ready to create a meal or entertain in style on short notice.

Here are just a few examples of the great variety of pasta salads:

- Pasta Salad Primavera (diced fresh vegetables)
- Pasta Pescatore Salad (fresh diced seafood)
- Pasta and Tuna Salad

- Pasta and Salmon Salad
- Pasta Salad al Pesto
- Pasta Salad California
- Pasta Salad Athena
- Pasta Salad with Curry Chicken
- Pasta Salad Italia
- Pasta Salad Peking
- Creamy Pasta Salad
- Pasta Salad Mexicana

FREEZING PASTA SALADS

Not only are pasta salads easy, light, and economical, but you can freeze the salads made with vegetables, chicken, meat, or pesto and small-shaped pasta. (Do not freeze seafood in a pasta salad; it gets dry and tasteless.)

Use plastic or glass bowls to freeze small portions of the salad. Cover tightly. Be sure to toss the pasta with a little vegetable or olive oil, unless it already has a sauce with an oil base.

Remove the pasta salad from the freezer and let it defrost for at least half an hour before serving. Toss the salad several times, adding more sauce if necessary.

You can even heat the pasta salad for a few minutes, adding some sauce or oil and tossing it through. To give the frozen pasta salad a really fresh taste and a burst of additional flavor, add more fresh herbs and vegetables or tomato sauce. Then serve the salad warm or at room temperature. This procedure ensures a full-flavored pasta salad and brings the pasta back to perfection.

For unscheduled entertaining or quick meals, microwave ovens work well for defrosting (but only for defrosting!).

Remember that fish and cheese sauces do not freeze well. But pesto, vegetable, tomato, or vinaigrette sauces work beautifully.

SOUP AND SALAD

The trend toward lighter eating in America has made the combination of soup and salad a favorite complete meal for lunch or dinner. In Italy, soup is also a popular way to serve pasta. There it is known as *Pasta in Brodo* (pasta in soup or broth). Soup is a meal in itself, or in smaller portions, a tasty and nutritious first course.

Italians are big soup eaters. They believe it is not only healthy, but good for the digestive system. Their soups are usually made with fresh vegetables and small pieces of pasta. This provides a nutritionally balanced meal-in-one which may be given added zest with a light sprinkling of Parmesan cheese.

Special pastas are made for soups—little circles, bows, wheels, and star shapes. Your Italian specialty store or supermarket will have a variety of them. Make Pasta in Brodo a regular part of your eating program and include it at least twice a week in your weight-loss diet menus. Check the menus for suggested soups.

Here are some tips for making soup:

- Avoid canned broths or consommé; they are full of salt and chemicals.
- Use packets of natural soup stock or consommé, which are available in health food stores.
- Frozen soups are also good.
- Use leftovers and add pieces of chicken, turkey, veal, or beef to vegetable soups.
- Best of all, use the Pasta Diet recipes to make your own soups from scratch. (Dice fresh vegetables with herbs and add chicken parts. Bring to a boil and then simmer for half an hour. Add small-shaped pasta and enjoy!)

10

Pasta and Sauces

There are three important facts to remember about making sauces for pasta: the quality of the products, the balance of the ingredients, and the texture of the sauce.

Sauces can be varied in thousands of different ways, depending on your individual taste, the occasion, and the preference of others, their dietary rules, or even their allergies (some people cannot eat onions; others are allergic to dairy products, etc.).

THE RIGHT KIND OF OIL

Because of the great variety of sauces and their versatility for pasta dishes, certain requirements are necessary to keep the sauce light, low-calorie, and wholesome. Rather than sacrificing taste, these requirements will enhance it, ensuring that the sauce will be delicious and satisfying.

The oil you use is, without question, of paramount importance. Choosing the right oil is as vital to the success of your recipe as choosing the freshest ingredients. Oil is as important in dieting and health as it is to the taste and texture of the sauce.

The green extra virgin first-pressing olive oil is the best, lightest, and tastiest. If this type is unavailable in your area look for imported olive oil; Pompei and Bertoli are among the better known brands that are widely distributed throughout America. If you can't find them at your local supermarket, they are sure to be in stock at specialty shops. The gourmet departments of department stores usually feature a wide selection of the finest imported olive oils, including the Italian green extra virgin olive oil.

The brand I prefer is called Raineri, from the Liguria region. I also favor the olive oils from the area of Florence and Tuscany in general.

Oil is preferred over butter for both dietary and health reasons. But, if you are making a sauce in which you would like to have a slight accent of butter, use 1 tablespoon of olive oil and 1 tablespoon of sweet (unsalted) butter. For certain recipes that require butter, use small amounts.

In Italy, olive oil (the fresh uncooked green extra virgin type) is added at the last minute on the top of salads, vegetable dishes, pasta sauces, and risottos.

Don't forget: The olive oil you use is just for coating, and not to make a sauce of oil. Use no more than 1–2 tablespoons for sautéing. It's against Italian culinary law to see oil in the bottom of the plate.

THE MAGIC OF VINEGAR

It used to be difficult, but it's happened at last. Today, you can go anywhere in America and find exciting blends of special European vinegars—the zesty mixes of herbs, fruits, spices, flowers, etc., that lend to each recipe a uniquely distinct taste.

The Pasta Diet stresses quality in all the ingredients, in the belief that delicious eating makes dropping weight easy. The Italian-style diet I've formulated is the incontestable proof that low-calorie meals need not be a trial. The vinegars recommended in the recipes are important to achieve the truly exciting flavor of some of the dishes. You'll be astonished to discover how a dash of the appropriate vinegar can even perk up your own old recipes.

It is generally thought that only salads require vinegar. That's far from true. Fish, chicken, liver, veal, rabbit, and quail are markedly enhanced by an application of the right type of vinegar. Vegetable dishes, such as Grilled Eggplant and Misto, also benefit from the zest of vinegar.

My own favorite vinegar is the balsamic from the area of Modena. I like to make my own vinegar with fresh herbs. It's actually rewarding to create a vinegar adapted to your own taste, choosing from among such herbs as tarragon, basil, mint, rosemary, or oregano.

I usually save old red wine, letting it sit out until it turns to vinegar. Red wine vinegar is preferred for salads or cooking. There is now available a sprightly raspberry vinegar which gives a perfect accent to sautéed chicken.

Lemon or apple cider vinegar is more easily digested by some people, though adding a small amount of the heartier vinegars can usually be tolerated. Keep two or three different varieties at your fingertips, varying them to give different accents to your recipes.

Note: If you mix vinegar with oil—safflower, olive, or vegetable—for your salads, use two parts of oil to one part of vinegar or lemon juice.

NO TO SALT

I believe that the American salt habit stems not from a national foible but from the flat, unexciting taste of much of the food we eat. Americans are the worst salt offenders in the world. They pick up a salt shaker before even tasting their food. (I often feel sorry for the poor chefs when I watch their creations being insulted by a shower of salt from an offending diner.)

Salt is bad for you. Sodium is not necessarily bad for you. All the sodium you need is contained in virtually all the food you eat which contains salt. There is enough *natural* salt in *natural food* to make it unnecessary to add salt when you cook. If you must, use sea salt in small amounts.

Everyone knows that salt contributes to increased blood pressure and is harmful to the heart and liver. It's even bad for the skin. Salt is also the enemy of any weight-loss diet, because it is a water-retainer. When water is held in the body tissues, it puffs up the cells, resulting in a sickly, bloated look which, in my opinion, is more unattractive than being overweight.

If you are a salt "fanatic," I recommend that you use instead the natural spices and herbs of the Pasta Diet. A dash of pepper added to the dish may help you get away from salt. Use spices like Spike, or All Seasons, Italian seasoning, or cayenne pepper. And don't be embarrassed to ask that your food be prepared without salt in restaurants—many people do. You will lose weight more quickly.

CHOOSING THE RIGHT CHEESES

Dairy products are generally not a part of any weight-loss diet, and with good reason. Except for the lowfat and low-salt varieties, dairy products have no place in the regimen of a conscientious weight reducer; and, in general, they should be consumed sparingly by anyone concerned with health and well-being.

Dairy products are high in calories. For many people, they are difficult to digest.

The worst insult you can give to a pasta sauce is to sprinkle it with one of the packaged grated cheeses. I've seen many a beautiful pasta sauce dealt a death blow by being sprinkled with these dairy products, which can be recognized by their sandy texture and unpleasant chemical taste.

On the Pasta Diet, you will learn to complement a fine sauce with a fine fresh cheese grated just before serving. Grating the cheese at the time you're making your sauce ensures that the cheese retains its strong taste. If you have your cheese grated at the time of purchase, store it in a plastic bag in the refrigerator.

Note: On the Pasta Diet, grated cheese is to be used sparingly because of its salt content. Even the few lowfat, low-salt cheeses recommended are always to be taken in small amounts. Cheese (mostly grated) is to serve as an "accent" to the sauce or pasta dish, *not* as a texture. And remember to avoid all creamy, cheddar, or prepared grated cheeses.

The cheese products recommended for the Pasta Diet weight-loss program are:

- Part skim mozzarella or low-salt mozzarella in water
- Lowfat or part skim ricotta
- Freshly grated Romano, Parmesan, or Pecorino. (Store chunks of the cheese coated in oil in jars with holes in the top for "breathing.")

WINE AND THE SAUCE

Cooking with wine adds a wonderful taste to the sauce; and, as you want this taste to enhance your sauce to the fullest, do not use the so-called cooking wines sold in the supermarkets. Do not use "cheap" wines, which are laden with chemicals, preservatives, and fillers. These wines add unnecessary calories to food and play havoc with your digestive system, and often result in those dull, heavy headaches.

I look upon wine as a food in itself, filled with vitamins, minerals, and important nutrients that aid digestion and help you relax. Be sure to choose dry white wine in sauces for "delicate" foods, such as fish, veal, white-meat chicken, as well as for quail and rabbit. Pastas with vegetables and fish are perfect with white wine.

(Red wine, being more complete because of the total fermentation process, lends a heavier, more robust taste to a sauce. It is best used in sauces for meat, lamb, and dark-meat chicken and in tomato-based sauces.)

Here are some of the most important Italian wines that can be purchased in restaurants and in your wine stores:

Light-Bodied Whites

Frascati
Gavi
Pinot Grigio
Torgiano
Riesling Italico

Dry Red Wines

Vino Nobile di
    Montepulciano
Gattinara
Amarone
Barbera
Barolo
Chianti Classico Reserva
Montepulciano d'Abruzzo
Rubesco
Valpolicella
Bonarda
Pezzalunga
Barbaresco

Medium-Bodied Whites
Fiano di Avellino
Greco di Tufo
Trebbiano d'Abruzzo
Orvieto
Verdicchio
Vernaccia di San Gimignano
Etna
Soave
Montanola

Don't believe the old wives' tale about grandmother's famous pasta sauce taking all day to cook. (Some people are still convinced they need to cook their tomato sauce all day!) Your own experience with the sauces of the Pasta Diet will surely give the lie to this old misleading adage. In fact, the reason the story got about was that in the old days in Italy, there being no proper stoves or heat to cook with, cooking generally was a protracted and time-consuming process.

The average time to cook all sauces is, in reality, no more than 8 to 10 minutes, sometimes less. And the basic steps are always the same: a large frying pan; a small amount of olive oil to start sautéing the ingredients; onions, garlic, etc.; herbs at the last minute—and *presto!*

To save time, make the sauce while the water is boiling for the pasta—and remember, don't overcook it!

11

"Just Desserts" for the Pasta Diet

Over the years, I have helped countless people lose weight rapidly and painlessly with the Pasta Diet. At first, before embarking on the program, they could hardly believe it. All these glorious, delicious foods, wines, and *desserts*, too?

For most people, desserts are the real obstacle to staying on a diet. The "sweet tooth" is the hardest tooth to resist, especially during a social dinner at home or at a restaurant. It's for this reason that the Pasta Diet includes recipes for suggested desserts. In the recipe section, you will find an appetizing array ranging from ice cream and cakes to fruit tarts and almond cookies.

If, when eating out or at a dinner party, you are served a dessert that you find hard to resist, follow these simple rules:

- Three tablespoons of anything will never hurt you.
- Take a taste to satisfy the craving—don't eat the whole thing.

The preferred types of dessert are: Ricotta cheesecake, fruits, ices, low-sugar almond cookies, fruit tarts, whipped or puréed frozen fruit desserts.

The desserts to select in restaurants, if you must, are: fruit tarts, meringues, sorbets, ices, fruit cakes, carrot cake, *ricotta* cheesecake.

My own two favorite desserts have also proven their success with conscientious dieters. I consider them so effective and satisfying that I will give them here as a foretaste of the delights to follow in the recipe section.

LUSCIOUS RICOTTA CHEESECAKE

Butter and flour for the pan
3   *large eggs*
3   *tablespoons flour*
1   *pound fresh part skim ricotta*
1/4 *cup sugar*
1/4 *teaspoon baking powder*
1/4 *cup grated lemon rind*
3   *tablespoons Amaretto, Nocello liqueur, or Grand Marnier
    (The accent of rum liquor may also be used.)*
1/4 *cup diced fruit, such as apricots, oranges, pineapple, or
    strawberries*

1. Butter and flour 6-cup springform.
2. Preheat the oven to 350 degrees.
3. Beat the eggs with the sugar in a large bowl. Add the ricotta and continue to beat. Slowly add the flour and baking powder; then add all the remaining ingredients, continuing to beat until smooth.
4. Pour the batter into the prepared pan and bake for 40 minutes, or until a toothpick inserted in the center comes out clean, and the cake has a light golden color.
5. Let the cake cool in the pan; then run a thin flexible knife or spatula around the pan to loosen the cake. Carefully

remove the rim of the springform and slide the cake onto a serving plate.

Ricotta cheesecake has a delicate texture, and many times it is best to serve the cake from the baking pan. Make sure the cake is well chilled before serving it either room temperature or slightly chilled in the refrigerator. Slice into even wedges and either sprinkle it with a dash of liqueur or serve it with fresh fruit.

Variation

You can vary the texture and taste by the fruits and liqueurs you use in the cake, or add a "nutty texture" by adding chopped almonds.

Time: 45 minutes
Servings: 6
Calories: 160 per 1/4-inch wedge

RASPBERRIES WITH ZABAGLIONE SAUCE

    3 medium-sized eggs
  1/2 cup sweet Marsala
    3 tablespoons prepared espresso coffee
    2 teaspoons sugar
  1/2 cup fresh raspberries per person

1. Separate the eggs. Beat the yolks lightly; then add the Marsala and coffee and beat until well combined.

2. Beat egg whites with the sugar until the meringue forms stiff peaks when the beaters are lifted. Gently fold the meringue into the egg-yolk mixture.

3. Divide the mixture among 4 small dessert bowls or glasses and sprinkle with the raspberries. Or place the raspberries on the bottom and the Zabaglione Sauce on top.

Variation

Zabaglione Sauce makes a delicious topping for strawberries, too.

Variations

Substitute strawberries, blueberries, or bananas for the raspberries.

Time: 10 minutes
Servings: 4
Calories: 110

12

Simple, Sensible, Relaxing: Exercise Italian-Style

The real joy of a reducing diet is to see your body change, becoming slimmer and more beautiful from day to day. As soon as you begin to incorporate exercise into your daily activities, you not only help hasten the achievement of your desired weight, but you will feel better right along. A few easy bends and stretches that can be done in less than 5 minutes at home or in the office, plus a *commitment to walking* whenever you can, will fulfill the moderate exercise needs you require.

In the Pasta Diet, I have included an exercise program cast in the Italian spirit—simple and sensible, relaxing to the mind as well as to the body. It will enable you to achieve maximum results in the minimum amount of time.

HOW IT'S DONE IN ITALY

Very few Italian women (or men) seemed to be running to a particular gym or exercise class. And yet the men and women were well proportioned. They had strong, healthy bodies. Cellulite "saddle bags" and large stomachs were virtually non-existent.

It was not at all mysterious. The secret begins with the Italian habit of eating small amounts of well-prepared, good-quality food. Most of the men and women I met have never been on any type of diet. Rather, they eat only at mealtimes and then many delicious courses in *small amounts*. Even restaurants serve about half of what American restaurants serve.

The secret really consists of the staple pasta, of which you can eat small amounts that satisfy the body and eliminate cravings. Pasta is fresh and natural without the chemicals that upset body metabolism.

The other part of the secret and probably the most important one is that Italians walk everywhere. Lack of physical activity is one of the chief reasons people get fat. Italians exercise for an hour or two each day without ever thinking about it. Walking is their main physical activity, followed by bicycling.

WHY EXERCISE?

Appearances, even slim appearances, can be deceiving. You can have perfect measurements and still have weak muscles, limited flexibility, and an inefficient cardiovascular system.

That's why I suggest you walk. It's an ideal exercise. It helps condition your body so that it functions more efficiently, which results in a higher energy level. The point of exercise is not how long it takes, or how much: It is exercising correctly with the right program.

The body needs different types of exercise. No one exercise or sport can make you fit. Only a combination can; that is, the combination of stretching, aerobic, and resistive exercises.

I often see people in health clubs and spas wasting time by doing the wrong exercises. The Pasta Diet offers a delicious, sound, versatile, and easy-to-prepare nutritional program. It will also tell you how to exercise correctly, and how to get the most out of your particular program in a short time.

DANGERS OF INACTIVITY

During the normal course of a day, most people do not exercise enough to keep their bodies attractive and healthy. It is easier and faster to drive instead of walk, to take elevators instead of climbing stairs, and to sit while doing simple tasks. Unfortunately, the age of "conveniences" has made us into a truly lazy society.

Inactivity not only results in the loss of muscle tone and elasticity, but causes stiffness of the joints, slowed-down circulation, glandular lethargy, and an accumulation of fats and toxins. The complexion and overall skin is affected. Hair, eyes, and energy levels are affected. And most important, the mental attitude about one's self is affected, the mind frame that affects one's success, both in the work sphere and in personal life.

Regular exercise should be designed to suit your body needs for toning and improvement. A few bends and stretches and an invigorating walk are beneficial both physically and mentally.

EXERCISE AND METABOLISM

Movement burns fat and the more you move, the less you will need to diet. (Another bonus: During vigorous exercise, a substance called glycerol is released into the bloodstream, which helps suppress the appetite.)

Dieting alone or consuming less than 600 calories slows down your metabolism or weight loss. Dieting leads to the loss of large amounts of lean tissue (muscle), causing you to look drawn. Protein in the muscle is needed for firm muscles. If you use too much of your own protein, you will decrease the lean mass, which is not the kind of weight you want to lose.

The scale tells us how much we weigh but not whether we have too much fat as compared to our weight being "lean mass" (muscle, bone, etc.).

THE SCALE IS NOT ALWAYS THE BEST JUDGE

Do not get overly concerned with what the scale says. The mirror should be your guide. Be concerned with how you look and feel and with healthy eating and exercising habits. You will first lose inches and become firmer rather than lose pounds. In the second stage, you have weight loss. The amount of loss varies with each person in accordance with individual body chemistry.

EXERCISE: THE "ENERGIZER"

Even though exercise uses up calories, it has the paradoxical effect of revitalizing and recharging inner energy. Interspersing the day with periods of physical activity keeps the real enervators—stress, inertia, low oxygen levels, slack muscles—from depleting your vigor before you're ready to refuel with sleep.

How can exercise give you back more energy than it takes?

For one thing, your body moves more efficiently when it is fit. The heart and lungs operate with less effort, thus requiring fewer calories to do the basic round-the-clock work. Another result is increased circulation, which distributes oxygen and nutrients to the cells more quickly, and that means renewed vitality. Joints stay flexible through constant use, work improves as tension eases and is replaced by a sense of well-being. All this conserves energy and allows you to use it more frugally.

The body takes time to get into shape. Thus, don't overestimate your fitness level at the outset. Begin by breaking up your workday with stretches, walking, and simple exercises. Then set aside time in the morning to do a specific exercise program that fits your body stamina and need.

10-POUND 14-DAY
MENU PLAN

Now that you've learned all about the Pasta Diet, you are ready to use my method to shed pounds deliciously and painlessly. I've structured a program in which pasta is incorporated once a day in your meal plans for rapid weight loss.

I've selected quick and easy-to-prepare recipes from my traditional home-style cooking, from those favored by celebrities and reducing spas, and from famous Italian restaurants in New York, San Francisco, and Los Angeles. My pasta recipes with all the marvelous trimmings will not only enable you to shed as much as 10 pounds in two weeks but, equally important, they will make you feel better, more energetic and healthier than you felt when you ate the high-fat, high-protein, high-cholesterol foods the average overweight person consumes.

I've been especially conscious in the Pasta Diet of the cholesterol issue. I've always known that pasta is a healthful food, but now surveys have confirmed beyond any doubt that such foods as my recipes emphasize are ideally low in cholesterol and high in nutritional necessities, such as fiber, carbohydrates, vitamins, and minerals. At last, the experts agree that something you really enjoy is good for you, too!

And here is the best news of all. This is a diet that need never be dull or repetitious. Variety is the spice of life, so many of the recipes I've included have been chosen for their adaptability. With these recipes as a basis, you will be able to create many new dishes and menus to make losing weight fun, fast, and delicious. For example, you can invent a dozen new dishes just by using my recipe for Stuffed Eggplant with Shrimp or Pasta Primavera, by varying the ingredients.

BREAKFAST

Of course you should eat breakfast!

Dieters often think it will help them lose weight faster if they skip that first meal of the day. But you need a balanced, nutritious start to give you solid energy for the morning hours. And there is another good reason to eat breakfast if you are on a diet: You won't get hungry if you eat three full meals daily.

I've selected some sample breakfast menus on the Pasta Diet to give you sound nutrition for the energy requirements of your daily tasks. You can match the individual breaksfasts with any lunch and dinner on the 14-day menu plan. They'll take no more than a few minutes to prepare, but I suggest that you take your time in eating. It is important to chew well and digest completely for that necessary "full" feeling.

Each breakfast contains complex carbohydrates, protein, and fat (a very small amount). Each item on the breakfast is designed with your overall health in mind. For instance, oatmeal reduces cholesterol, rye builds muscle, and the entire program stabilizes blood sugar.

Like the lunches and dinners on the Pasta Diet, the breakfasts emphasize freshness and taste. There is fruit to give you that zingy wake-up feeling and light items such as tofu (with cinnamon) or oatflakes to give you the sense of being comfortably full. None of the breakfasts is over 200 calories.

BREAKFAST

Mix and match with any of the lunches and dinners.

I.
1 medium-sized apple
2 ounces part skim ricotta
   or 2 poached eggs
   or 1 cup oatmeal
1 slice rye toast

III.
1 medium-sized orange
2 ounces oatflakes
   sprinkled with raisins
   and sunflower seeds
   cinnamon
1/2 cup skim milk

II.
1/2 cup raspberries, or 1 cup
   strawberries
1 slice whole wheat toast
4 ounces lowfat cottage
   cheese

IV.
1/2 papaya, or 1 medium-
   sized peach
4 ounces plain yogurt
   sprinkled with raisins
   and sunflower seeds
1 rice cake

For variety, choose from the following and exchange with any of the items suggested in the breakfast plan—fruit for fruit, grain item for grain item.

orange juice, 1 cup	110
bran flakes	105
espresso or herb tea	00
whole wheat toast	60
grapefruit, 1/2	50
cantaloupe, 1/2	60
applesauce, 1/2 cup	100
peach	35
fresh fruit cocktail, 1/2 cup	100
grapefruit juice, 1 cup	95
banana	100
2 poached eggs	160
2 scrambled eggs	190
(1 teaspoon sweet [unsalted] butter)	
1 cup oatmeal (made with water)	80

PASTA DIET 14-Day Menu Plan

≈≈ Day One ≈≈

LUNCH

Italian Bean Salad
Pasta with Creamy Pesto Sauce
Cold Lemon Gelata

DINNER

Tomato, Spinach, and Mushroom Soup
2 RyKrisps
Baked Fish with Almonds
1 cup broccoli

≈≈ Day Two ≈≈

LUNCH

Tomato and Zucchini Soup
RyKrisp
Eggplant, Pepper, and Pasta Salad
3 fresh apricots

DINNER

Antipasto with Cucumber Dill Dip
Stuffed Eggplant with Shrimp
Italian Green Beans with Herbs
Fresh raspberries with 1 tablespoon Framboise

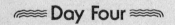 Day Three

LUNCH

Tossed Green Salad with Vinegar
Macaroni Seafood Misto
1 cup unsweetened applesauce

DINNER

Zucchini and Broccoli Salad
Baked Eggplant Lillo-Concordia, London
Chicken Sergio
Pineapple Cream al Lynn

Day Four

LUNCH

Salad Greens with Vinegar Dressing
Pasta Primavera Celli
1/2 cup diced fresh fruit

DINNER

Tomato Zucchini Soup
Italian Bean Salad
Lasagne with Ricotta-Meat Sauce alla Trevor

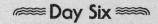

Day Five

LUNCH

Mozzarella and Tomato Salad
Seafood Vegetable Misto alla Jilly
Fresh peach or strawberries

DINNER

Vegetable Torta Celli
Chicken with Mushrooms and Wine
Cold Apricot Gelata "Monica"

Day Six

LUNCH

Gazpacho
Rigatoni alla Guiseppe
Poached Pear

DINNER

Minestrone Soup
2 slices Pizza (Amazing 300-Calorie Pizza)
Mixed tossed salad
Lemon, oil herb dressing

≈≈ Day Seven ≈≈

LUNCH

Zucchini Misto
Eggplant Rolls Stuffed with Pasta
or
Seafood Pasta Salad
1 cup green grapes

DINNER

Antipasto with 5 tablespoons Cucumber Dressing
Tomato, Spinach, and Mushroom Soup
Lasagne with Chicken with Tomato Sauce
1 cup Mixed Salad—Lemon, oil herb dressing

≈≈ Day Eight ≈≈

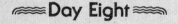

LUNCH

Gazpacho
2 RyKrisps
Green Fettucine with Cheese Sauce alla Sinatra
1 cup strawberries

DINNER

Mama Celli's Misto
Stir-Fry Chicken Italian Style
Mixed Salad
1 medium apple

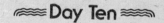

Day Nine

LUNCH

Asparagus-Stuffed Eggs
Poached Fish alla Livornese
Mixed Green Salad

DINNER

4 RyKrisps
Eggplant Dip
Pasta with Clam Sauce alla J.D.
Pineapple with Kirsch

Day Ten

LUNCH

Tossed Salad Greens with Lemon Dressing
Macaroni Misto Roberto
1/2 cup fresh raspberries

DINNER

Italian Vegetable Stew
Eggplant Parmigiana
Lamb in Mushroom and Tomato Sauce
Cold Lemon Gelata

≈ Day Eleven ≈

LUNCH

Green Vegetable Misto
Pasta and Salmon Salad
Fresh pear

DINNER

Artichoke Caponata
Tossed Green Salad with Lemon Dressing
Veal Limone Mancini
Strawberries with Zabligione Sauce

≈ Day Twelve ≈

LUNCH

Tossed Green Salad with Cucumber Dressing
Venetian Fish Stew
Apple

DINNER

Artichoke and Mushroom Salad
Linguine with Chicken Sauce
Grapefruit and Banana Ice

≈≈ Day Thirteen ≈≈

LUNCH

Vegetable Salad Ischia
Fish Soup Abruzzi Style
Spaghetti with Eggplant Sauce Sala
Fresh peach or pear

DINNER

Green Vegetable Misto
Mushroom Salad
Braised Lamb in Wine
Strawberry Fluff Amaretto

≈≈ Day Fourteen ≈≈

LUNCH

Vegetable Salad
Stuffed Eggplant Nousha
Shrimp in Garlic Sauce
Fruit Purée

DINNER

Artichoke Mushroom Salad
Veal Chops Sala
1/2 cup cooked brown rice
1 slice Ricotta Cheesecake

DAY ONE

ITALIAN BEAN SALAD

1 *pound fresh Italian green beans*
1 *pound fresh wax beans*
1 *shallot, peeled*
1 *garlic clove, peeled*
2 *tablespoons vegetable oil*
1 *tablespoon red wine vinegar*
1 *teaspoon Italian seasoning*
2 *tablespoons minced fresh Italian parsley leaves*

1. Trim and wash the green and wax beans, and cut them into 1-inch lengths. Steam the beans over 1 1/2 cups of water for 6 minutes. Then plunge into cold water until the beans are cool and drain well. The beans should still be crunchy. Transfer the beans to a salad bowl.

2. Mince the shallot into a small bowl. Put the garlic through a press into the same bowl. Add the oil, vinegar, and Italian seasoning to the bowl. Mix the dressing well; then pour it over the beans and toss. Sprinkle the salad with the parsley and serve.

Time: 15 minutes
Servings: 6
Calories: 85 per serving

PASTA WITH CREAMY PESTO SAUCE

    8 ounces pasta (Capellini, linguine, or short macaroni are the
       best pastas for this sauce.)
    1 cup chopped fresh basil leaves (in season)
  1/4 cup chopped fresh Italian parsley leaves
    2 garlic cloves, crushed
    3 tablespoons extra virgin olive oil
    3 tablespoons freshly grated Parmesan cheese

1. Bring a large covered pot of water to boil to cook the pasta.

2. Put the basil and parsley leaves and garlic in a blender container. Blend for 2 seconds. Start adding the oil 1 teaspoon at a time, blending for 1 second after each addition until all the oil is blended in. Add the Parmesan cheese and blend thoroughly. If the mixture is dry, add 3 tablespoons of warm water.

3. When the pasta is ready, drain and put it into a warm serving bowl into which you have poured some Pesto Sauce. Toss thoroughly, add the remaining sauce, and blend thoroughly. Serve immediately.

Variations

If you can't find fresh basil leaves, use fresh spinach leaves. You will, of course, have a completely different taste and not the original Italian classic Pesto.

For a creamy version, add 1/4 cup part skim ricotta.

For a more "liquidy" Pesto Sauce, add 1/4 cup of the pasta cooking water and toss the pasta with a little olive oil first. Then toss it with the cheese (which you have not added to the blender) and toss with the sauce.

Three tablespoons pignolis (pine nuts) can also be blended into the sauce.

Time: 10 minutes
Servings: 4
Calories: 290 per 4-ounce portion with pasta

OLD LEMON GELATA

    2 teaspoons unflavored gelatin
1/4 cups skim milk
    2 eggs, separated
1/4 cup fresh lemon juice
    2 teaspoons Grand Marnier
    2 teaspoons grated lemon rind

1. Soften the gelatin in the milk in a large saucepan or the top of a double boiler.

2. Beat the egg yolks until lemon colored. Add the lemon juice and Grand Marnier and stir the mixture into the milk. Place over low heat or hot water and cook, stirring, until the gelatin is dissolved and the mixture thickens. Remove from the heat and cool. Add the lemon rind.

3. Beat the egg whites until stiff. Carefully fold the egg whites into the cooled lemon mixture. Spoon into a 4-cup bowl or soufflé dish and chill until firm. Serve with fresh fruit if desired.

Time: 10 minutes, excluding time for chilling

Servings: 8

Calories: 45 per serving

TOMATO, SPINACH, AND MUSHROOM SOUP

    1 *pound ripe plum tomatoes*
  3/4 *pound fresh spinach*
  1/4 *pound fresh mushrooms*
    1 *garlic clove, peeled*
  1/2 *teaspoon freshly grated nutmeg*
    1 *cup water*

1. Bring a saucepan of water to a boil. Remove the core from the tomatoes and drop the tomatoes into the boiling water. Remove from the heat and let the tomatoes sit in the water for 2 to 3 minutes. Then transfer them to a bowl of cold water and let them sit in the cold water for 2 to 3 minutes, or until the skins begin to pucker. Peel the tomatoes and squeeze out the seeds. Chop the tomatoes. There should be about 2 cups.

2. Wash the spinach thoroughly, removing the stems and any damaged leaves. Cook the spinach in the water clinging to the leaves for 4 minutes. Drain well and chop the spinach. There should be 1 cup.

3. Wash and trim the mushrooms and chop them. There should be 1/2 cup.

4. Put all the vegetables into a saucepan and push the garlic through a press into the mixture. Add the nutmeg and water. Cover the pan and simmer over medium-low heat for 10 minutes.

Time: 15 to 20 minutes
Servings: 4 (scant 1 cup each)
Calories: 85 per serving

BAKED FISH WITH ALMONDS

    4 fresh trout, 1 to 1 1/2 pounds each
    1 tablespoon vegetable oil
    1/2 cup dry white wine
    1/4 cup chopped fresh Italian parsley leaves
    1/4 cup blanched slivered almonds
    3 lemons, cut into very thin slices and seeded

1. Have your fish monger scale and dress the trout. The heads can be removed or not as you please.

2. Preheat the oven to 400 degrees.

3. Coat a baking dish with the oil and arrange the trout in the dish in a single layer.

4. Mix the wine and parsley and spoon the mixture over the fish. Spoon the almonds evenly over the fish and arrange the lemon slices on top. Bake for 20 minutes and serve immediately.

Time: 25 minutes
Servings: 4
Calories: 305 per serving

DAY TWO

TOMATO AND ZUCCHINI SOUP

    1 pound ripe plum tomatoes
    3 shallots, peeled
    4 zucchini (about 5 ounces each)
    1/3 cup chopped fresh Italian parsley leaves
    1/3 teaspoon Italian seasoning
    1 cup water
       Grated Romano cheese

1. Bring a saucepan of water to a boil. Remove the cores from the tomatoes and drop the tomatoes into the boiling water. Remove from the heat and let the tomatoes sit in the water for 2 to 3 minutes. Then transfer them to a bowl of cold water and let them sit in the cold water for 2 to 3 minutes, or until the skins begin to pucker. Peel the tomatoes and squeeze out the seeds. Cut the tomatoes into 6 pieces each and drop the pieces into a blender container.

2. Chop the shallots into the tomatoes and blend for a few seconds to make a purée.

3. Scrub and trim the zucchini but do not peel them. Chop the zucchini into small pieces.

4. Put purée, zucchini, parsley, Italian seasoning, and water in a saucepan. Cover and cook over medium heat for 10 minutes, or until the zucchini is as tender as you like it. Sprinkle 1 tablespoon of grated Romano cheese over each serving if you like.

Variation

For a perfectly smooth texture, the zucchini can also be puréed in the blender along with the tomatoes and shallots.

Time: 20 minutes
Servings: 6 (scant 1 cup each)
Calories: 40 per serving

EGGPLANT, PEPPER, AND PASTA SALAD

Serve as a salad or first course; or turn into a serving bowl, garnish with pitted ripe olives, and serve with crackers or toast squares as cocktail food. You can also spoon the salad onto large tomato slices as an accompaniment to a cold poultry or meat dish. Great pasta salad as is!

1   pound swirl-shaped pasta
1   2-pound eggplant
3   tablespoons olive oil
1/4   cup red wine vinegar
2   medium-sized sweet green peppers
3   large sweet red peppers
1/3   cup minced fresh Italian parsley leaves
4   plum tomatoes
3   garlic cloves, peeled
1/4   teaspoon cayenne pepper, or to taste

1. Fill a large pot with cold water. Bring to a boil over high heat. Add salt, if desired. Then add the pasta and cook, stirring occasionally, just until the pasta is *al dente*. Drain the pasta in a colander and rinse it with cold water and drain again.

2. Preheat the broiler.

3. Wash the eggplant and trim off the ends. Cut the eggplant lengthwise into halves and put the halves cut side up on a baking sheet brushed with a few drops of the oil. Sprinkle 1 tablespoon of the vinegar on each cut surface and broil for 15 minutes.

4. Trim the green and red peppers, discarding the ribs and seeds. Cut the peppers into quarters. Place skin side up on the baking sheet with the eggplant halves and broil until

the skin is blistered. Remove the eggplant and pepper from the broiler and set aside until cool enough to handle.

5. While the eggplant cools, rub off the skins of the peppers with a coarse cloth. Rinse the peppers, chop them into small pieces, and put the pieces into a large bowl.

6. Discard the eggplant skin and put the pulp through a food mill into the bowl with the peppers. Add the parsley to the bowl.

7. Wash the tomatoes and cut out the hard part around the stem of each tomato. Squeeze the tomatoes gently to get rid of as many seeds as possible. Chop the tomatoes and add them to the bowl.

8. Add the remaining oil and vinegar to the bowl. Push the garlic through a press into the mixture. Mix with a wire whisk until everything is blended. Add as much of the cayenne as you like. Add the pasta and mix well.

Time: 30 minutes

Servings: 16 (1/2 cup per salad serving)
(32 appetizer servings)

Calories: 50 per 1/2 cup

RAW VEGETABLE ANTIPASTO

Vegetables can make an attractive centerpiece as well as a perfect first course. Your guests will delight in such an appetizing beginning—light, tasty, not fattening, and very healthy. Use any of the raw fresh vegetables listed and arrange them in baskets or crystal bowls or on oval serving platters.

Mushrooms, sliced thin
Fennel strips
Cherry tomatoes
Zucchini, thin rounds or sticks
Asparagus tips
Broccoli flowerets

Radishes
Cucumber slices or sticks
Carrot sticks
Cauliflower flowerets
String beans

If you have never eaten raw asparagus, broccoli, cauliflower, or string beans, this will be a new taste experience for you. Serve with the Cucumber Dill dip that follows or any of these:

Ricotta and Mustard Dip
Curry Dip
Eggplant and Garlic Dip
Oil, Lemon, Herb Dip
Tomato-Avocado Dip

CUCUMBER DILL DIP

This recipe is a close relative to the Cold Cucumber Soup, but the proportions of liquid to solid are different.

    1 young cucumber, or 2 smaller cucumbers (10 ounces total weight)
  1/4 cup skim milk
  1/2 cup lowfat cottage cheese or part skim ricotta, or more to taste
    2 tablespoons snipped fresh dill
    1 tablespoon snipped fresh chives
    1 tablespoon Dijon mustard
       Pinch of cayenne pepper

1. Peel and dice the cucumber.
2. Combine all the ingredients in a blender container, and blend at low speed for 3 seconds. Switch to high speed for 3 seconds. Continue to add more cheese until the dip is as thick as you like it. Adjust the amounts of herbs to suit your taste.
3. Chill the dip; it will thicken further as it cools. Makes about 2 cups.

Time: 10 minutes, excluding time for chilling
Servings: 8–10
Calories: 5 per tablespoon

EGGPLANT STUFFED WITH SHRIMP AND PASTA

1/2 *pound short-shaped pasta*
2 *tablespoons vegetable oil*
2 *1-pound eggplants*
1 *pound fresh mushrooms*
1 *pound raw shrimp in shells*
1 *onion (4 ounces), peeled*
2 *garlic cloves, peeled*
1/4 *cup chopped fresh Italian parsley leaves*
1/2 *cup dry white wine*
1/4 *teaspoon Italian seasoning*

1. Fill a large pot with cold water. Bring to a boil over high heat. Add salt, if desired. Then add the pasta and cook, stirring occasionally, just until the pasta is *al dente.* Drain the pasta in a colander and rinse it with cold water and drain again. Transfer the pasta to a bowl and toss it with the oil.

2. Wash the eggplants and remove the stems and leaves, but do not peel them. Cut the eggplants lengthwise into halves, and carefully scoop out the pulp without damaging the shells. Poach the shells in a large pot of water for 5 minutes; then turn them upside down to drain.

3. Wash and trim the mushrooms, dry them on paper towels. Then chop the mushrooms into coarse pieces.

4. Shell and devein the raw shrimp, and then chop them.

5. Brush a large baking dish with a few drops of the oil.

6. Preheat the broiler.

7. Heat the remaining oil in a large frying pan. Chop the onion into the oil and push the garlic through a press into the pan. Add the mushrooms and the scooped-out eggplant

pulp. In about 5 minutes, when the onion is translucent and the other vegetables just tender, add the chopped shrimp, 2 tablespoons of the parsley, the wine, and Italian seasoning. Cook for another 5 minutes, stirring often to mix.

8. Put eggplant shells in the oiled baking dish and fill them with the shrimp mixture. Sprinkle the tops with the rest of the parsley and the cheese.

9. Run under the broiler for a few minutes, or until cheese is golden brown. Serve 1 eggplant half for a main dish. Cut each half again into halves for a first-course serving.

Variations

Instead of mushrooms and white wine, use 1 pound of ripe plum tomatoes. Wash them, remove the cores, and chop the tomatoes into small pieces. Add to chopped eggplant pulp and cook until just tender.

Other filling possibilities are diced cooked meat or chicken or mixed vegetables.

Time: 20 minutes
Servings: 4 as main dish, 8 as first course
Calories: 200 per main-course serving

ITALIAN GREEN BEANS WITH HERBS

     1   pound Italian broad, flat green beans
     1   tablespoon olive oil
     4   shallots, peeled
     2   tablespoons minced fresh basil leaves
    1/2 teaspoon crumbled dried oregano
     2   tablespoons fresh lemon juice
     3   tablespoons chopped fresh Italian parsley leaves

1. Wash beans, and snip off the tops and tails. Cut the beans diagonally into 1 1/2-inch pieces. Put the beans in a large saucepan, cover with cold water. Bring to a boil, and cook for 5 to 8 minutes, or until the beans are barely tender. They should still be crunchy. Drain the beans and rinse them under cold water or plunge them into a pan filled with cold water. Drain again.

2. Heat the oil in a frying pan and mince the shallots into the hot oil. Sauté until they are translucent. Stir in the basil and oregano and cook for 1/2 minute. Then add the beans to the pan and sauté, turning the beans until they are coated with the oil and herbs. Add the lemon juice and parsley and heat through. Serve at once.

Variations

This recipe works well for string beans too; they can be used whole.

Add minced fresh dill or minced garlic or sprinkle with freshly ground black pepper just before serving.

Note: If you must resort to frozen beans, this way of preparing them will greatly enhance their flavor.

Time: 15 minutes
Servings: 4
Calories: 60 per serving

DAY THREE

MACARONI SEAFOOD MISTO

This recipe is ideal for using up an assortment of leftovers.

1 pound pasta (penne, ziti, elbows, or shells)
1 large sweet green pepper
1 onion (3 ounces)
2 tablespoons vegetable oil
1 garlic clove, peeled
2 celery stalks, chopped
1/2 cup chopped cooked vegetables
    (zucchini, red pepper, mushrooms)
1 cup tomatoes, chopped (fresh or imported plum tomatoes)
or 5 chopped or diced olives
1/4 cup chopped fresh Italian parsley leaves
1 cup chopped cooked seafood
1/3 teaspoon Italian seasoning

1. Fill a large pot with cold water. Bring to a boil over high heat. Add salt, if desired. Then add the pasta and cook, stirring occasionally, just until the pasta is *al dente*. Drain the pasta in a colander and turn the pasta into a 2-quart casserole. Set aside until needed.

2. While the pasta cooks, make the sauce: Wash and trim the green pepper, discarding the ribs and seeds. Chop the pepper. Peel and chop the onion. There should be 1/2 cup.

3. Heat the oil in a large saucepan and push the garlic through a press into the hot oil. Add the onion, green pepper, and celery, and cook for a few minutes, or until the onion is translucent. Add the cooked vegetables, tomatoes, olives, parsley, seafood, and seasoning. Cook until well mixed and hot; then simmer for a few minutes longer.

4. Preheat the oven to 350 degrees.

5. Pour the sauce mixture over the pasta in the casserole

and mix gently but thoroughly with wooden spoons. Bake for 8 to 10 minutes, or until cooked to your taste.

Time: 25 minutes
Servings: 10
Calories: 250 to 300 per serving, depending on choice of seafood and vegetable for sauce

ZUCCHINI AND BROCCOLI SALAD

This dish is great for buffets.

1 pound fresh broccoli
4 unwaxed zucchini (about 1 pound total weight)
4 pimientos, drained
3 scallions, trimmed
1 bunch watercress, washed and dried
3 tablespoons vegetable oil
5 tablespoons red wine vinegar
2 teaspoons minced fresh tarragon
3 tablespoons minced fresh dill
2 medium-sized unpeeled red apples
Juice of 1/2 lemon

1. Wash and drain the broccoli. Break off the broccoli flowerets and slice them into a large bowl. (Use the rest of the broccoli for something else.)

2. Scrub the zucchini and score them lengthwise with the tines of a fork. Cut the zucchini into thin round slices. Add the slices to the broccoli.

3. Slice the pimientos and scallions into the bowl.

4. Break the watercress leaves from the stems and add the leaves to the bowl. (Save the watercress stems for stock or soup.)

5. In a cup, mix the oil, vinegar, tarragon, and dill to make a dressing. At serving time, toss the dressing with the vegetables.

6. Cut the apples into very thin slices and dip them into the lemon juice to prevent discoloration. Arrange the apple slices around the top of the salad.

Variation

If you prefer, blanch or steam the broccoli and zucchini for 3 to 5 minutes; then refresh them in cold water and drain before starting to make the salad. This method requires about 15 minutes more to make the dish.

Time: 6 minutes
Servings: 6
Calories: 125 per serving

BAKED EGGPLANT LILLO-CONCORDIA

1 1-pound eggplant
   Oil
1 pound ripe plum tomatoes
3 shallots, peeled
1/4 cup chopped fresh Italian parsley leaves
1 garlic clove, peeled
3 tablespoons freshly grated Parmesan cheese

1. Cut the eggplant into 1-inch thick slices, and soak the slices in cold water for 1/2 hour to remove bitter taste. Drain and pat dry. Put the slices on a lightly oiled pan and broil for 5 minutes on one side. Set aside.

2. Bring a saucepan of water to a boil. Remove the cores from the tomatoes and drop the tomatoes into the boiling water. Remove from the heat and let the tomatoes sit in the water for 2 to 3 minutes. Then transfer them to a bowl of cold water and let them sit in the cold water for 2 to 3 minutes, or until the skins begin to pucker. Peel the tomatoes and squeeze out the seeds. Chop the tomatoes. There should be 2 cups.

3. Preheat the oven to 350 degrees. Pour 2 tablespoons of oil into a small frying pan and heat. Chop the shallots into the pan and add the parsley. Push the garlic through a press into the mixture. Sauté until the shallots become translucent. Add the tomatoes and cook until the mixture is thick.

4. Pile the vegetable mixture on the unbroiled side of the eggplant slices, and sprinkle each one with grated cheese. Bake for 15 minutes. Serve with a vegetable accompaniment or appetizer.

Time: 30 minutes

Servings: 6

Calories: 110 per serving

CHICKEN SERGIO

    4 *boneless and skinless chicken halves (5 ounces each)*
    3 *sprigs Italian parsley*
  1/2 *pound fresh mushrooms*
  1/2 *cup dry white wine*
    6 *shallots, peeled*
  1/2 *teaspoon minced fresh tarragon*
  1/4 *cup drained capers*
    3 *tablespoons Dijon mustard*
       Freshly ground black pepper

1. Wipe the chicken breasts with a cloth dipped into cold water; then pat them dry. Flatten the breast pieces slightly with the flat side of a cleaver.

2. Wash and dry the parsley and cut off the stems. Wash the mushrooms and trim off the bottom of the stems.

3. Pour 1/4 cup of the wine into a heavy frying pan, and place over medium-to-low heat.

4. Chop the shallots into the wine and then slice the mushrooms into the pan. Stir with a wooden spoon. Snip the parsley into the pan and add the tarragon and capers.

5. Slash the chicken breast pieces across the top and bottom and add them to the pan. Cook for 2 minutes.

6. Mix the remaining wine with the mustard and black pepper to taste and pour the mixture over the chicken. Turn the chicken and check the inside, where the slashes are, to help with the timing. Cook just past the pink stage to keep the chicken tender, about 8 minutes altogether. If the liquid in the pan evaporates, add a little more white wine and keep turning the chicken until it is done to your taste.

7. Serve on warmed plates, with the pan sauce on top, and sprinkle with a little freshly ground pepper. Accompany with rice and a green vegetable.

Variations

Add more mustard or wine or capers to your taste. Keep tasting the sauce as you cook to be sure the taste is just right.

Omit the capers or mushrooms.

Instead of tarragon, use 3 sprigs of fresh dill, snipped.

Serve cold, garnished with lots of fresh dill.

Time: 10 minutes
Servings: 4
Calories: 210 per serving

PINEAPPLE CREAM AL LYNN

1 1/2   pounds fresh pineapple
    3   tablespoons Grand Marnier
        Juice of 1/2 lemon
  1/4   cup part skim ricotta

Peel and trim the pineapple and cut it into small pieces. Mix everything in a large bowl until smooth. Cover and chill before serving.

Variations

Blender method: Process all the ingredients together in a blender until a very smooth sauce is formed. Use as a sauce, spooned over cake or a fruit dessert. Or chill in individual serving dishes and serve as a dessert on its own.

Canned, unsweetened crushed pineapple can be used if fresh pineapple is not available.

Diced strawberries or strawberry or raspberry purée can be added for color.

Plain yogurt can be substituted for the ricotta.

Note: The amount of fresh pineapple needed for this recipe, about 2 cups after dicing, is about half of the average market pineapple. You can use the entire pineapple to make a double recipe and store the balance of the recipe in the refrigerator or freezer for another occasion.

Time: 10 minutes
Servings: 4
Calories: 80 per serving

DAY FOUR

PASTA PRIMAVERA CELLI

1 *pound pasta (thin spaghetti, green spinach noodles, homemade pasta, or other very thin pasta)*
1 *pound zucchini*
1 *pound ripe plum tomatoes, or 3 pounds canned imported Italian plum tomatoes, drained*
4 *large fresh mushrooms*
3 *tablespoons vegetable oil*
6 *shallots, peeled*
1/4 *cup chopped fresh Italian parsley leaves*
2 *tablespoons minced fresh basil leaves, or 1 tablespoon dried basil*
2 *small garlic cloves, crushed and peeled*
1 *tablespoon Italian seasoning*
1/2 *cup chopped broccoli flowerets*
    Pinch of cayenne pepper
1/4 *cup freshly grated Parmesan cheese*

1. Fill a large pot with cold water. Bring to a boil over high heat. Add salt, if desired. Then add the pasta and cook, stirring occasionally, just until the pasta is *al dente*. Drain the pasta in a colander and return it to the pot while it is still hot.

2. While the pasta is boiling, wash and trim the zucchini, tomatoes, and mushrooms, but do not peel them.

3. Pour the oil into a large skillet, but do not yet put the pan over the heat.

4. Dice the unpeeled zucchini and tomatoes into the oil; then dice in the shallots. Slice the mushrooms into the mixture and add the parsley. Add the basil. Crush or purée the garlic into the pan; then add the Italian seasoning, chopped broccoli, and pepper.

5. Turn on the heat to medium-high and cook, while stirring often with a wooden spoon. (Use your own

judgment as to when the sauce is ready, but it should be cooked in 8 to 10 minutes. If you want a smoother sauce, you can cook it longer, or even purée it, but Primavera is best when there is a slight texture in the vegetables, so that you can chew and identify each one.)

6. Pour the sauce over the pasta, a small amount at a time, and toss with two wooden forks to mix before adding more. Add half of the Parmesan cheese, and toss again. Taste, and add more salt and pepper, if necessary. Serve immediately in heated small soup dishes or pasta bowls. Serve the remaining cheese in a separate bowl, to be added according to individual taste.

Variations

Omit the mushrooms and broccoli. Add chopped eggplant, green peppers, pignolis (pine nuts), almonds, pimientos, or asparagus. For a creamy texture, add 1/4 cup part skim ricotta during final moments of cooking the sauce.

Time: 15 minutes

Servings: 8

Calories: 235 per serving of pasta, sauce, and cheese

LASAGNE WITH RICOTTA-MEAT SAUCE ALLA TREVOR

```
       1 pound lasagne noodles
     1/2 pound ripe plum tomatoes
10 to 12 shallots
       2 tablespoons vegetable oil
       1 clove garlic, peeled
     1/4 pound ground lean beef, lamb, or veal
     1/4 cup chopped fresh Italian parsley leaves
       1 cup part skim ricotta
```

1. Fill a large pot with cold water and bring to a boil. Add the noodles, one or two at a time, so the water does not stop boiling. Cook the noodles until slightly firmer than *al dente*, then remove from the heat and carefully arrange them on a towel.

2. While the noodles cook, prepare the sauce: Wash the tomatoes and remove the cores. Chop the tomatoes. There should be 1 cup.

3. Peel and mince the shallots. There should be 1/2 cup.

4. Heat the oil in a large frying pan. Push the garlic through a press into the hot oil. Add the shallots and sauté until they are translucent. Add the ground meat and parsley and sauté until the meat is no longer pink, a few minutes. Stir in the tomatoes and cook for 8 minutes. If necessary add more seasoning to taste.

5. Preheat the oven to 350 degrees.

6. Use a flat 2-quart lasagne dish. Spoon a thin layer of the sauce in the pan, then arrange a layer of noodles, another layer of sauce, and about half of the ricotta. Make a second layer of noodles, sauce, and ricotta, and finish with the rest of the sauce.

7. Bake for 8 to 10 minutes, or until done to your taste. Let sit for a few minutes, then cut into squares to serve.

Time: 25 minutes
Servings: 8
Calories: 335 per serving

1/2 cup dry white wine
1 1/2 teaspoon Italian seasoning
1/4 cup chopped fresh Italian parsley leaves

DAY FIVE

MOZZARELLA AND TOMATO SALAD

    4 large firm ripe tomatoes (1 1/2 pounds total weight)
    1 pound part skim mozzarella
    1 tablespoon olive oil
    2 tablespoons chopped fresh basil leaves
    2 tablespoons chopped fresh Italian parsley leaves

1. Wash and core the tomatoes and cut them into thin slices.

2. Cut the mozzarella into slices of the same shape.

3. Arrange the tomato slices on 6 plates and sprinkle oil over the tomato slices. Arrange the cheese slices on the plates and sprinkle the basil and parsley over all.

Time: 5 minutes
Servings: 6
Calories: 80 per serving

SEAFOOD VEGETABLE MISTO ALLA JILLY

    1 pound striped bass, flounder, or other white-fleshed fish
       fillets, or 1 pound shelled and deveined shrimps or shelled
       mussels or scallops
    1 large sweet green pepper
    2 tablespoons oil
    1 garlic clove, peeled
    3 shallots, peeled
  1/4 cup chopped celery
  1/4 teaspoon hot red pepper flakes
  1/2 cup dry white wine
  1/2 teaspoon Italian seasoning
  1/4 cup chopped fresh Italian parsley leaves

1. Dice the fish fillets into 1/2-inch pieces. If the shrimp or scallops are large, they can be split or chopped.

2. Wash the green pepper and discard the ribs and seeds. Chop the pepper.

3. Heat the oil in a large saucepan and push the garlic through a press into the hot oil. Chop shallots into the pan and add the celery, green pepper, and hot red pepper. Sauté and stir together for 3 minutes.

4. Add the fish or shellfish, wine, and Italian seasoning and mix well. Cook for 5 minutes. Serve sprinkled with the chopped parsley.

Variations

Add chopped mushrooms or chopped zucchini or substitute the mushrooms and zucchini for the celery and green pepper. You can also use chopped broccoli and diced pimientos as substitutions or additions.

Time: 15 minutes
Servings: 4
Calories: 215 per serving (based on striped bass)

VEGETABLE TORTA CELLI

    1   pound assorted vegetables, such as eggplant, sweet peppers,
        and zucchini
    1/2 pound ripe plum tomatoes
    6 to 8 shallots
    2   tablespoons olive oil
    2   garlic cloves, peeled
    1/3 cup chopped fresh Italian parsley leaves
    1/2 teaspoon hot red pepper flakes
    1/3 teaspoon Italian seasoning
    3   tablespoons chopped fresh basil leaves
    4   ounces part skim mozzarella

1. Wash and trim the vegetables, peel if necessary, and cut them into thin slices. There should be at least 2 cups.

2. Wash the tomatoes and remove the cores. Chop the tomatoes. There should be 1 cup.

3. Peel and chop the shallots. There should be 1/3 cup.

4. Use a few drops of the oil to coat a 6-cup baking dish (a 9-inch-deep pie dish is a good choice). Pour the rest of the oil into a frying pan.

5. Push the garlic through a press into the oil and add the shallots, part of the parsley, and the red pepper flakes. Sauté until the shallots are translucent; then add the tomatoes, Italian seasoning, basil, and remaining parsley. Cook, stirring often, until the mixture is reduced to a sauce.

6. While it cooks, preheat the oven to 350 degrees and chop or shred the cheese.

7. Layer all the ingredients in the baking dish, vegetables, tomato sauce, cheese, then another layer of each, ending with the cheese. Bake for 15 minutes. Cut into wedges to serve.

Time: 30 minutes
Servings: 4
Calories: 185 per serving

CHICKEN WITH MUSHROOMS AND WHITE WINE

1 cup dried black mushrooms (about 2 ounces)
2 2 1/2-pound frying chickens
1 white onion (4 ounces)
1/2 pound ripe plum tomatoes or 2 cups canned imported Italian plum tomatoes
1 teaspoon olive oil
3/4 cup dry white wine
1/3 cup chopped fresh Italian parsley leaves
3 tablespoons chopped fresh basil leaves

1. Soak the mushrooms in hot water while preparing the other ingredients.

2. Cut the chickens into pieces, dividing the half breasts into 2 portions. Save the backs and necks for stock. Remove all skin.

3. Peel and chop the onion.

4. Wash the tomatoes and remove the cores. Chop the tomatoes.

5. Heat the oil in a frying pan and add the chopped onion. Sauté until the onion is translucent. Brown the chicken pieces on all sides in the same pan.

6. Add the wine, parsley, basil, and tomatoes.

7. Drain the mushrooms, remove the stems (save for something else), and cut the caps with scissors into thin slivers.

8. Add the mushrooms to the mixture, cover pan, and cook for 10 minutes, or until the chicken is done to your taste.

Time: 25 minutes
Servings: 8
Calories: 225 per serving

COLD APRICOT GELATA "MONICA"

1 7-gram envelope unflavored gelatin
1 cup skim milk
2 eggs, separated
1 cup puréed cooked fresh apricots
2 tablespoons Grand Marnier
1 teaspoon almond extract

1. Soften the gelatin in the milk in a large saucepan.
2. Beat the egg yolks until they are lemon-colored; then add them to the milk.
3. Place the pan over low heat or barely simmering hot water and cook, stirring, until the gelatin has dissolved and mixture thickens. Remove from the heat and cool.
4. Add the puréed apricots, Grand Marnier, and almond extract.
5. As the mixture begins to set, beat the egg whites until stiff. Carefully fold the beaten egg whites into the apricot mixture.
6. Spoon into a 4-cup bowl or soufflé dish or mold, cover, and chill until firm. Serve plain or with additional apricot purée mixed with Grand Marnier.

Time: 10 minutes, excluding time for chilling
Servings: 8
Calories: 60 per serving (without additional purée
           or Grand Marnier)

DAY SIX

GAZPACHO

    3 large tomatoes
    1 medium-sized cucumber
    1 medium-sized onion
    1 large sweet green pepper
    1 garlic clove
  3/4 cup tomato juice
    3 tablespoons white wine vinegar
    2 tablespoons olive oil
       Juice of 1 lemon
  1/2 teaspoon Dijon mustard
  1/4 teaspoon cayenne pepper
    6 tablespoons chopped watercress leaves
    6 lemon wedges

1. Wash and peel the tomatoes and remove the cores. Wash and trim the cucumber.

2. Peel the onion.

3. Wash and trim the green pepper and discard the ribs and all seeds. Chop all these vegetables into small pieces and turn them into a large bowl.

4. Peel the garlic and push through a press into the vegetables. Add to the bowl the tomato juice, vinegar, oil, lemon juice, mustard, and cayenne. Mix well; then purée in a blender, half or less at a time, until smooth. Mix all the batches together.

5. Serve cold, with watercress leaves on top and a lemon wedge with each serving.

Time: 20 minutes, excluding time for chilling
Servings: 6
Calories: 105 per serving

RIGATONI ALLA GUISEPPE

1 1 1/2-pound eggplant
1 pound rigatoni
2 tablespoons olive oil
2 garlic cloves, crushed and peeled
1/4 cup minced fresh basil leaves
1/4 cup minced fresh Italian parsley leaves
2 tablespoons freshly grated Parmesan cheese

1. Wash and trim the eggplant, but do not peel it. Cut it lengthwise into halves. Soak the eggplant halves in cold water to cover with 1 tablespoon salt per quart of water for 15 minutes. Drain, rinse, drain again, and pat dry. Cut the unpeeled eggplant into very thin slices, then cut the slices into 1/4-inch-thick strips.

2. While the eggplant is soaking, bring a large pot of water to a boil. When rapidly boiling, add the rigatoni and 1 tablespoon salt and cook for 10 minutes, or until done to your taste.

3. While the pasta cooks, heat the oil in a large frying pan and push the garlic through a press into the pan. Add the eggplant strips and sauté them with the garlic, turning to cook all the pieces evenly.

4. When the rigatoni is cooked, drain and turn into a pasta bowl. Sprinkle with the herbs and cheese and toss to mix. Top with eggplant strips which have been drained on paper towels, toss again gently, and serve. Add more grated cheese if you like.

Note: In the original dish, the cheese used is ricotta salata. If you can find this salted, pressed ricotta, try it instead of Parmesan.

Time: 20 to 25 minutes
Servings: 8
Calories: 275 per serving of pasta, sauce, and cheese

MINESTRONE SOUP

1 cup dried beans, such as navy, kidney, red, garbanzo,
   or a mixture
1 cup fresh string beans
2 tablespoons minced garlic
1 small zucchini, diced
1 cup shredded spinach or cabbage
1 cup diced tomatoes
1 cup finely diced carrots
1 cup chopped onion
1 cup chopped celery
1/2 cup finely chopped parsley leaves
1/2 teaspoon Italian seasoning
12 ounces tomato juice
2 tablespoons extra virgin olive oil
3/4 cup elbow macaroni

1. To prepare the dried beans, first soak them overnight
in 2 quarts of cold water. After soaking, place beans in pot
with 2 cups water, cover, and boil for 1 hour. Save the
cooking liquid.

2. In another large pan, sauté all of the vegetables in the
oil.

3. Place half the beans in a blender and purée. Add all
the ingredients, except the macaroni, to a large pot. Add the
2 cups of bean liquid and bring to a boil. Simmer for 45
minutes to 1 hour. Then add the macaroni and simmer for 15
minutes, or until the macaroni is tender. Add water to thin,
if necessary.

Time: 2 hours
Servings: 10 1-cup servings
Calories: 150

AMAZING 300-CALORIE PIZZA

The secret to calorie-cutting in this pizza is using egg whites instead of lots of white flour. Egg whites are more healthful and less caloric. This switch slims a standard 12-inch diameter crust to a mere 300 calories.

    8   egg whites, lightly beaten
    1/2 cup whole wheat flour
    1   tablespoon freshly grated Parmesan cheese
    1/4 teaspoon Italian seasoning
    1/4 teaspoon garlic powder
        Toppings

1. Preheat the oven to 350 degrees. Combine all ingredients in a bowl. Blend and pour into greased 12-inch-diameter pizza pan.
2. Bake for 12 minutes.
3. Cool slightly for 2 to 3 minutes and spread with tomato sauce, diced mozzarella (part skim), and other desired toppings: mushrooms, peppers, olives, etc.
4. Return to oven and bake for 7 to 8 minutes, or until the cheese is bubbly.
5. Serve as an appetizer, main course with a salad, or snack with wine—diced into small pieces.

Note: Vary the toppings according to the occasion, guests, and what you have to work with. It's great for using up leftovers.

Keep the calories down by not using anchovies, pepperoni, salami, sausage, or other meats. Best with cheeses and vegetables. Can also be served white (without the tomato sauce), using only vegetables, or just sprinkled with freshly ground black pepper and used as a bread.

Time: 30 minutes
Servings: Makes 6 slices
Calories: 300 per serving

DAY SEVEN

ZUCCHINI MISTO

    3   zucchini (about 5 ounces each)
    8   ripe plum tomatoes
    2   medium-sized sweet green peppers
    1   large onion (4 ounces)
    4   large fresh mushrooms
    2   tablespoons vegetable oil
  1/2   teaspoon Italian seasoning
    3   tablespoons dry red wine
    1   cup shredded lettuce, or 4 Bibb lettuce leaves
        Pinch of freshly ground black pepper
        Minced fresh Italian parsley leaves

1. Scrub the zucchini and trim them. If they are fresh and unblemished, do not peel them.

2. Wash the tomatoes and peppers. Remove the ribs and seeds from the peppers.

3. Peel the onion. Chop all these vegetables.

4. Wash and dry the mushrooms, trim the stems, and cut the mushrooms into slices.

5. Pour the oil into a large frying pan. Add all the chopped vegetables, the sliced mushrooms, Italian seasoning, and a pinch of freshly ground black pepper. Sauté over medium heat, stirring often, until the peppers are tender, about 6 minutes.

6. Add the wine and continue to cook for 5 minutes longer. Season with salt to taste. Serve warm or chill and serve on a bed of shredded lettuce or in a perfect Bibb lettuce leaf. Sprinkle each serving with parsley.

Variation

Serve hot. In this case, you may prefer to sprinkle cheese on top just before serving.

Time: 15 to 20 minutes
Servings: 6
Calories: 85 per serving

Choose either the Eggplant Rolls or Seafood Pasta Salad for lunch.

EGGPLANT ROLLS STUFFED WITH PASTA

    2 large 1 1/2-pound eggplants
    2 garlic cloves, crushed
  1/4 cup chopped onions
    3 tablespoons extra virgin olive oil
    1 pound ripe plum tomatoes, diced
  1/4 cup chopped fresh Italian parsley leaves
  1/2 teaspoon Italian seasoning
  1/2 cup red wine vinegar
    1 pound small elbow macaroni
  1/4 cup freshly grated Parmesan cheese

1. Wash and trim the eggplants, and cut off a 1/4-inch slice from each end. Then cut the remaining eggplant into 1/4-inch-thick slices. Soak in cold water with salt for 10 minutes and rinse twice. Drain on paper towels.

2. Preheat the broiler.

3. Sauté the garlic and onions in the oil with tomatoes, parsley, and Italian seasoning for 10 minutes.

4. Put the eggplant slices on a baking dish, sprinkle with the vinegar, and brown in the broiler for 3 to 5 minutes.

5. Preheat the oven to 350 degrees.

6. Cook the pasta in boiling water until *al dente* and drain. Add the pasta to the tomato sauce (save 1 cup of sauce for the topping) and mix the pasta and sauce thoroughly.

7. Use two shallow baking dishes and rub with oil. Put about 2 to 3 tablespoons of the pasta mixture in the center of each eggplant slice and fasten with a toothpick. Line all the eggplant rolls in the baking dish and pour the remaining sauce on top and sprinkle with Parmesan cheese.

8. Bake for 10 minutes. Can be served hot or room temperature.

Time: 30 minutes
Servings: 48 eggplant rolls
           24 servings for appetizers
Calories: 80 calories per roll

SEAFOOD PASTA SALAD

For large groups the ingredients can be increased to make more servings; it is an excellent dish for a buffet. Although this is a perfect first course, it can serve as a main dish or as a salad.

    1   pound small pasta shapes
    2   tablespoons vegetable oil
    6   fresh mussels in shells
   12   raw shrimp in shells
   1/2   cup diced fresh raw squid
   1/2   cup cooked fresh crab meat
    3   pimientos, drained
    6   shallots, peeled
   1/3   cup chopped fresh Italian parsley leaves
   1/4   cup chopped celery
    1   garlic clove, peeled
    2   tablespoons red wine vinegar
         Juice of 2 lemons
   1/4   teaspoon Italian seasoning

1. Fill a large pot with cold water. Bring to a boil over high heat. Add salt, if desired. Then add the pasta and cook, stirring occasionally, just until the pasta is *al dente*. Drain the pasta in a colander and rinse it with cold water and drain again. Transfer the pasta to a bowl and toss it with the oil.

2. Scrub the mussels, remove their beards, and steam over a small amount of water until the shells open, about 4 minutes. Remove the mussels from the shells and place them in a bowl.

3. Poach the shrimp in enough water to cover until the shells turn pink, about 5 minutes. Remove the shells, devein the shrimp, if necessary. Chop shrimp into 1/2-inch pieces. Add to the mussels.

4. Poach the squid pieces in water to cover for 2 or 3 minutes. (Do not overcook the squid or it will toughen.) Drain the squid and add it to the mussels and shrimps. (All the steaming and poaching steps can be done at the same time.) Add the crab meat. Let all the seafood cool.

5. Chop the pimientos and shallots into a large salad bowl. Add parsley and celery, and push the garlic through a press into the vegetables. Add the cooled seafood and the pasta and toss to mix. Then pour in the vinegar and lemon juice. Add Italian seasoning and salt and pepper to taste. Toss again to mix well and serve well chilled.

Time: 30 minutes
Servings: 6
Calories: 115 per serving

LASAGNE WITH CHICKEN-TOMATO SAUCE

  1 1/2 *pounds lasagne noodles*
      1 *pound ripe plum tomatoes*
      8 *fresh mushrooms*
      1 *onion (2 ounces)*
      1 *large sweet green pepper*
      2 *tablespoons vegetable oil*
         pinch of cayenne pepper
      2 *cups diced cooked chicken*
    1/3 *teaspoon Italian seasoning*
    1/3 *cup chopped fresh Italian parsley leaves*

1. Fill a very large pot with water and bring to a boil. Add the noodles, one or two at a time so the water does not stop boiling. Cook the noodles until they are slightly less

than *al dente;* then remove from the heat and carefully arrange them on a towel.

2. While noodles cook, prepare the sauce: Wash the tomatoes and remove the cores. Chop the tomatoes. There should be 2 cups.

3. Wash and trim the mushrooms and chop them. There should be 1/2 cup.

4. Peel and mince the onion. There should be 1/4 cup.

5. Wash and trim the pepper, discarding the ribs and seeds. Chop the pepper.

6. Heat the oil in a large frying pan and sauté the chicken and vegetables for a few minutes, or until the chicken is lightly browned. Add the tomatoes, cayenne pepper, and Italian seasoning, and cook for about 10 minutes.

7. Preheat the oven to 350 degrees.

8. Use a deep 3-quart round baking dish. Spoon a thin layer of sauce in the bottom; then add a layer of noodles. (You may need to trim noodles to fit them into the round pan.) Spoon some sauce over the noodles; then sprinkle on some Parmesan cheese. Continue making layers until you have about 5 layers of noodles and 5 layers of sauce. Top with the rest of the sauce and cheese.

9. Bake for 8 to 10 minutes, or until done to your taste. Let the dish set and cool slightly before cutting into wedges. Sprinkle the parsley around the edge. This is an excellent dish for buffet service.

Time: 30 minutes

Servings: 12

Calories: 310 per serving

DAY EIGHT

GREEN FETTUCINE WITH CHEESE SAUCE ALLA SINATRA

1 pound green fettucine noodles
2 cups part skim ricotta
1/2 cup skim milk
3 tablespoons freshly grated Parmesan cheese
1/4 cup chopped fresh basil leaves

1. Fill a large pot with cold water. Bring to a boil over high heat. Add salt, if desired. Then add the fettucine and cook, stirring occasionally, just until the pasta is *al dente*. Drain the pasta in a colander.

2. Meanwhile, mix the ricotta with the milk and Parmesan cheese. Add the basil to the cheese mixture and stir through until smooth and creamy.

3. Put the cheese mixture in a saucepan and stir for 5 minutes over low heat. When warm and smooth, remove from heat and toss with the green fettucine noodles. Add more grated Parmesan cheese, if desired.

Time   10 minutes
Servings: 8
Calories: 260 (3-ounce serving)

MAMMA CELLI'S MISTO

    2 *large sweet green peppers*
    1 *large sweet red pepper*
    2 *white onions (3 ounces each)*
    3 *zucchini (4 ounces each)*
    3 *tablespoons vegetable oil*
    2 *eggs*
  1/4 *cup chopped fresh Italian parsley leaves*
    3 *tablespoons freshly grated Parmesan cheese*

1. Wash the peppers and cut them into halves. Discard the stems, ribs, and seeds. Chop the peppers or cut them into slivers.

2. Peel and chop the onions.

3. Wash and trim the zucchini, but do not peel them. Dice the zucchini.

4. Heat the oil in a frying pan and add the peppers and onions. Sauté until the onions are translucent. Add the zucchini and cook for a few minutes.

5. Beat the eggs and parsley together and season with salt and pepper. Pour the eggs into the vegetable mixture with one hand while stirring rapidly with a fork with the other. Mix everything well. Cook for a few minutes, or until the eggs are set. Sprinkle with the cheese and serve immediately. Use as an appetizer, or as a main course accompanied by a salad and fruit and cheese.

Variations
This misto can be made without the eggs.
Other vegetables can be substituted.

Time: 20 minutes
Servings: 6
Calories: 135 per serving

STIR-FRY CHICKEN ITALIAN STYLE

1 1/2   *pounds boneless and skinless chicken breast*
   2   *sweet red or green peppers*
   3   *tablespoons olive oil*
   2   *tablespoons minced garlic*
1/4   *teaspoon hot red pepper flakes*
1/4   *cup chopped onion*
1/2   *cup diced broccoli, string beans, bean sprouts, mushrooms, snow peas, or celery (your choice), cut into 1/4-inch pieces*
1/2   *cup dry white wine*

1. Cut the chicken into 1/4-inch pieces.
2. Wash and seed the peppers and cut them into 1/4-inch pieces.
3. Heat 2 tablespoons of the olive oil with 1 tablespoon of the minced garlic in a wok or large frying pan. Add the chicken and sprinkle with the hot pepper flakes. Stir-fry for 1 to 2 minutes. Remove the chicken and set it aside.
4. Heat the remaining oil and garlic. Add all the vegetables and toss to mix. Stir-fry to the texture you desire; then add the wine and the chicken and cook for a few minutes. Serve with brown rice and add Parmesan cheese as a topping.

Variations
Use fish, veal, or beef and a variety of vegetables.

Time: 30 minutes
Servings: 4
Calories: 395 per serving

DAY NINE

ASPARAGUS-STUFFED EGGS

    6   fresh asparagus
    4   hard-boiled eggs
1/4   cup fresh lemon juice
    1   teaspoon minced fresh tarragon
    1   garlic clove, crushed and peeled
    1   pimiento, drained and cut into strips

1. Wash and trim the asparagus; then break off the tough bottom portion of the stalks. Blanch or steam the asparagus for 5 to 6 minutes. Drain well.

2. Shell the eggs and cut them lengthwise into halves.

3. Put the yolks into a blender container with the asparagus, lemon juice, tarragon, and garlic. Blend for a few seconds, until reduced to a purée.

4. Stuff the egg whites with the purée and garnish them with the pimiento strips.

Time: 10 minutes
Servings: 4 (2 halves per serving)
Calories: 90 per serving

POACHED FISH ALLA LIVORNESE

2 pounds boneless fish fillets, such as red snapper, sole, or striped bass
1 pound ripe plum tomatoes, or 2 cups canned imported Italian plum tomatoes, chopped
2 tablespoons vegetable oil
4 shallots, peeled
1/4 cup dry white wine
3 tablespoons drained capers
4 sprigs fresh Italian parsley, chopped

1. Cut the fish into 6 portions, rinse, and pat them dry.
2. Wash the tomatoes and remove the cores. Chop the tomatoes. There should be about 2 cups.
3. Heat the oil in a large frying pan. Mince the shallots into the oil and sauté until they are translucent.
4. Put fish pieces in the pan in a single layer and add the wine and capers. Cook for 2 minutes.
5. Add the tomatoes, parsley, and salt and pepper to taste. Cover the pan and poach the fish for 6 to 10 minutes. After 6 minutes, check the fish with a fork. Cook fish only until it is white and tender; do not overcook.

Variations
Add sliced mushrooms, eliminate tomatoes, or add dill weed.

Time: 25 minutes
Servings: 4
Calories: 260 per serving

EGGPLANT DIP

1 1 1/2-pound eggplant
2 tablespoons olive oil
1 garlic clove, peeled
6 shallots, peeled
3 tablespoons chopped fresh Italian parsley leaves
2 tablespoons fresh lemon juice
   Freshly ground black pepper

1. Preheat the broiler.
2. Peel the eggplant and cut it into small cubes. Put the cubes in a single layer on a baking sheet and sprinkle them with 1 tablespoon of the olive oil. Broil for 5 minutes. Remove from the broiler and let the cubes cool.
3. Heat the remaining olive oil in a small frying pan and push the garlic through a press into the oil. Chop the shallots into the pan and add the parsley. Sauté for 2 minutes.
4. Put the eggplant cubes and the shallot mixture into a blender container. Add the lemon juice and blend for a few seconds, or until the mixture is smooth. Season with salt and pepper to taste.
5. Cover and chill until ready to serve. Serve on crackers, small wheat rounds, or cubes of rye or wheat Italian bread. Also with low-calorie, raw vegetables. Makes about 2 1/2 cups.

Variations

Serve the dip on inch-long sections of celery stalks or on whole Belgian endive leaves or stuff cherry tomatoes with the purée.

Vary the spread by adding diced sweet green peppers or chopped ripe black olives.

Time: 10 minutes, excluding time for chilling
Servings: 12 or more (3 tablespoons each)
Calories: 30 per tablespoon

PASTA WITH CLAM SAUCE ALLA J.D.

    1/2 pound linguine
      2 dozen fresh minced clams or 1 cup canned clams
      2 tablespoons vegetable oil
    2–3 garlic cloves, peeled and crushed
      3 shallots, peeled
    1/2 cup chopped fresh Italian parsley leaves
    1/2 cup dry white wine
    1/4 cup freshly grated Parmesan cheese
         Freshly ground white pepper

1. Fill a large pot with cold water. Bring to a boil over high heat. Add salt, if desired. Then add the pasta and cook, stirring occasionally, just until the pasta is *al dente*. Drain the pasta in a colander.

2. Put the clams in a bowl and cover with cold water. Soak for 5 minutes. Then open the clams. Do this over a bowl to save the juices. Strain juices to remove any sand.

3. Heat the oil in a frying pan. Push the garlic through a press into the hot oil. Dice the shallots into the oil and add the parsley. Sauté for a few minutes.

4. Put the opened clams and strained juices in a small saucepan and add the wine. Simmer for 5 minutes, then add the clams and liquid to the sautéed vegetables and cook for 1 or 2 minutes to mix well.

5. Add the drained pasta to the sauce, and toss and heat for 1 minute.

6. Pour over the pasta and cook and toss. Sprinkle with Parmesan cheese and white pepper and serve at once.

Time: 20 minutes
Servings: 4
Calories: 280 per serving of pasta and sauce

PINEAPPLE WITH KIRSCH

    1 3-pound fresh pineapple
    1/2 cup kirsch
        Juice of 1 lemon

1. Discard the peel and core of the pineapple, and cut the flesh into chunks. There should be at least 4 cups. Put the pineapple in a glass or pottery bowl.

2. Heat the kirsch with the lemon juice to blend the flavors. Cool. Pour the mixture over the pineapple chunks and let the fruit macerate for 30 minutes or longer. Toss several times. Serve plain or spooned over plain cake or ice cream.

Time: 10 minutes, excluding time for macerating
Servings: 8
Calories: 80 per serving

DAY TEN

LEMON DRESSING
(For Salads, Fish, and Cold Veal)

6 *tablespoons fresh lemon juice (about 2 lemons)*
2 *tablespoons olive oil*

Pour the lemon juice and oil into a cup or small bowl and mix with a whisk until emulsified. Pour the dressing over salad and toss well. Makes 1/2 cup.

Variation
Add minced fresh herbs, such as basil, parsley, or the herb of your choice, to the dressing before spooning it over the salad.

Note: The proportions of lemon juice to oil can be changed to taste, but the calorie count will change accordingly.

Time: 5 minutes
Servings: 6 (4 teaspoons each)
Calories: 48 per 4 teaspoons

MACARONI MISTO ROBERTO

1 *pound of mixed pasta shapes and colors (green, red, and yellow colors, with shapes of penne, ziti, elbows, and shells)*
3 *tablespoons olive oil*
1 *large sweet green pepper, diced*
6 *shallots, diced*
2 *garlic cloves, minced*
2 *small zucchini, diced*
1/2 *cup diced fresh mushrooms*
1/2 *cup diced celery*
1/4 *teaspoon Italian seasoning*
2 *cups diced ripe plum tomatoes, or canned imported Italian plum tomatoes*
1/2 *cup diced black olives*
1/4 *cup diced fresh Italian parsley leaves*
3 *tablespoons freshly grated Pecorino cheese*

1. Fill a large pot with cold water. Bring to a boil over high heat. Add salt, if desired. Then add the pasta and cook, stirring occasionally, just until the pasta is *al dente*. Drain the pasta in a colander.

2. Heat the oil in a large saucepan. Add the pepper, shallots, garlic, zucchini, mushrooms, and celery to the pan and sauté for 8 minutes, stirring often.

3. Add the tomatoes and Italian seasoning and cook for 10 minutes.

4. Add the parsley and chopped olives. Toss the sauce with the drained pasta. Sprinkle with cheese and toss again. Serve immediately.

Time: 25 minutes
Servings: 10
Calories: 250 calories (4-ounce serving)

ITALIAN VEGETABLE STEW

>2 *pounds assorted fresh vegetables, such as broccoli,*
>   *carrots, celery, eggplant, mushrooms, onions, sweet*
>   *peppers, potatoes, tomatoes, or zucchini*
>1 to 1 1/2 *cups water or chicken stock (page 185) or veal stock*
>   *(page 186)*
>1/3 *cup chopped fresh Italian parsley leaves*
>   3 *tablespoons chopped fresh basil leaves*
>1/4 *teaspoon crumbled dried marjoram*
>   2 *teaspoons olive oil*
>   3 *tablespoons freshly grated Parmesan cheese*

1. Wash the vegetables and trim or peel them if necessary. Cut the vegetables into medium-sized pieces, as uniform as possible.

2. Put 1 cup of the water or stock into a large saucepan. Use the rest of the liquid if necessary. This will depend on the size and shape of the saucepan and the vegetables in the mixture: carrots and potatoes need more liquid; celery and mushrooms less.

3. Add to the saucepan any vegetables that need longer cooking (carrots, peppers, or potatoes) and cook for 2 minutes.

4. Add the rest of the vegetables and simmer for 6 to 8 minutes longer, or until they are done to your taste. However, all vegetables taste better when they are cooked *al dente*.

5. Stir in all the herbs and the oil. Season with salt and pepper to taste. Serve hot or cold with 1/2 tablespoon of Parmesan cheese sprinkled over each serving. This is delicious with brown rice.

Time: 20 minutes

Servings: 6

Calories: 85 per serving (This varies with the choice of vegetables and does not include the rice.)

EGGPLANT PARMIGIANA

Many Italian eggplant dishes start with sautéing the slices. While it can be done, fresh eggplant absorbs a great deal of oil and a large amount is needed for sautéing. The broiling method, which is used for other eggplant recipes in this book, gives more tender, more delicious eggplant with many fewer calories. Serve as an appetizer, a main course, or as an accompaniment to a main course.

    1 1 1/2-pound eggplant
       Salt
    2 tablespoons olive oil
  1/2 pound ripe plum tomatoes
    3 shallots, peeled
    2 tablespoons chopped fresh Italian parsley leaves
    2 tablespoons chopped fresh basil leaves
  1/4 cup freshly grated Parmesan cheese
    2 ounces part skim mozzarella

1. Preheat the broiler.
2. Wash and peel the eggplant and cut it lengthwise into thin slices. Soak the slices in cold salted water for a few minutes; then rinse in fresh cold water until the water is clear. Pat the slices dry.
3. Brush a few drops of the olive oil on a baking sheet and arrange the eggplant slices on the sheet in a single layer. Broil for 5 minutes, set aside.
4. Meanwhile, wash and core the tomatoes and chop them. There should be about 1 cup.
5. Preheat the oven to 350 degrees.
6. Heat the remaining olive oil in a small frying pan and chop the shallots into the pan. Sauté for 1 minute; then add the herbs and tomatoes. Cook for 10 minutes, stirring occasionally. Spoon the sauce into a large baking dish.
7. Arrange the eggplant slices on top of the sauce in a single layer. Sprinkle with the Parmesan cheese.
8. Cut the mozzarella into thin slices and then into strips. Arrange the strips over the eggplant. Bake for 15 minutes.

Variations

Mushrooms or ground lean beef can be added to the tomato sauce. You can make a form of eggplant lasagne by adding 2 to 3 more layers.

Time: 30 minutes
Servings: 6
Calories: 135 per serving

LAMB IN MUSHROOM AND TOMATO SAUCE

2   *pounds boneless lamb cubes from the shoulder or leg*
1/2 *pound ripe plum tomatoes*
1   *tablespoon vegetable oil*
2   *shallots, peeled*
1   *garlic clove, peeled*
2   *tablespoons Italian seasoning*
1   *cup sliced fresh mushrooms*
1/2 *pound fresh okra*
    Freshly ground black pepper
2   *tablespoons freshly grated Parmesan cheese*

1. Cut all fat off the lamb and flatten the cubes with the flat side of a cleaver.

2. Bring a saucepan of water to a boil. Remove the cores from the tomatoes and drop the tomatoes into the boiling water. Remove from the heat and let the tomatoes sit in the water for 2 to 3 minutes. Then transfer them to a bowl of cold water and let them sit for 2 to 3 minutes, or until the skins begin to pucker. Peel the tomatoes and squeeze out the seeds. Chop the tomatoes. There should be about 1 cup.

3. Pour the oil into a large frying pan with a cover. Chop the shallots and garlic into the pan. Add the Italian seasoning, mushrooms, and lamb pieces and sauté over brisk heat until the lamb pieces are lightly browned. Add the chopped tomatoes and simmer for a few minutes.

4. Meanwhile, wash the okra carefully and cut off the little caps at the stem ends. Chop the okra into 1/2-inch pieces. Add the okra to the pan with black pepper to taste, and cook for 3 minutes longer.

5. Preheat the oven to 350 degrees.

6. Spoon the sauce into a 6-cup casserole dish and sprinkle the cheese on top. Bake for 12 minutes. (Or continue cooking in the frying pan. Add the cheese, cover the pan, and cook for 8 minutes.)

Note: Meat labeled "lamb stew" can come from the shoulder or leg, but may also come from the neck, flank, or breast. For lean pieces, try to buy shoulder or leg so you can be sure to have boneless lean cubes that will cook quickly. Both portions are flavorful, but the leg will generally cost more.

Time: 20 minutes
Servings: 6
Calories: 380 per serving

DAY ELEVEN

GREEN VEGETABLE MISTO

    1   pound fresh spinach
1 1/2   pounds fresh broccoli
    2   tablespoons olive oil
    6   shallots, peeled
    3   garlic cloves, peeled
    3   tablespoons chopped fresh basil leaves
  1/4   cup chopped fresh Italian parsley leaves
  1/4   teaspoon freshly grated nutmeg
  1/4   cup part skim ricotta
  1/4   teaspoon dry mustard

1. Wash the spinach well, discarding any damaged leaves and all the stems. Use scissors to cut the leaves into small pieces. There should be about 2 cups.

2. Wash and drain the broccoli, and separate the flowerets. (Use the stems for another dish.) Chop the flowerets.

3. Heat the olive oil in a large frying pan. Mince the shallots into the oil and push the garlic through a press into the oil. Add the spinach and broccoli and sauté, turning until all the vegetables are coated with oil. Cover the pan and steam for 5 or 6 minutes.

4. Uncover the pan and mix in the basil, parsley, and nutmeg. Season with salt and pepper to taste.

5. Mix the ricotta and dry mustard together in a cup; then turn into a blender container and whirl for 1 second. Add the vegetable mixture to the container and blend for 3 or 4 seconds.

6. Serve at room temperature, or return to the skillet and reheat to serve hot. Use as vegetable accompaniment to a main course, or serve as a sauce. Makes about 4 cups.

Variations

Add 1 cup chopped ripe plum tomatoes, asparagus, celery, or zucchini.

The Misto can also be used as a filling for tomatoes or fish rolls.

Time: 15 to 20 minutes
Servings: 8 as a vegetable; 16 as a sauce
Calories: 65 per serving; 8 per 1 tablespoon

PASTA AND SALMON SALAD

Many different kinds of seafood can be used in this salad, even canned tuna; also various kinds of crustaceans. Try shrimp, mussels, clams, small squid, lobster, or use a mixture of several kinds.

    1 cup chopped or flaked cooked fresh salmon, or canned
       salmon, or other cooked seafood
  1/3 cup chopped celery
  1/3 cup chopped fresh Italian parsley leaves
 8–10 shallots, peeled and minced
  1/4 cup drained, chopped pimiento
    1 cup cooked pasta (elbows, ziti, penne, or pieces of spaghetti)
    2 tablespoons vegetable oil
       Juice of 1 lemon
  1/3 teaspoon dry mustard
  1/4 cup chopped fresh dill

1. Put the fish in a large bowl and add the celery, parsley, shallots, and pimiento. Mix well. Add the pasta and toss gently.

2. Mix the oil, lemon juice, and mustard in a cup until the mustard is dissolved. Mix in dill and pour the sauce over the fish and pasta. Chill for a few minutes before serving.

Variations

Add chopped olives, green peppers, tomatoes, or hard-boiled eggs. Or substitute any of these for one of the other ingredients.

Time: 15 minutes
Servings: 4
Calories: 225 per serving

ARTICHOKE CAPONATA

This makes an excellent appetizer, but it can also serve as a vegetable to accompany a main course, and it can be served as a sauce with pasta.

    2   cooked large fresh artichokes (see Note)
    2   white onions (1 ounce each)
    2   tablespoons olive oil
    2   garlic cloves, peeled
  1/2   cup dry white wine
    3   tablespoons drained capers
  1/3   teaspoon crumbled dried oregano

1. When the artichokes are cool enough to handle, remove all remaining leaves and the choke. Cut bottoms into small pieces. There should be 1 cup.

2. Peel and mince the onions. There should be 1/4 cup.

3. Heat the oil in a frying pan and push the garlic through a press into the oil. Add the onions and diced artichokes, and sauté for 4 minutes.

4. Add the wine, capers, and oregano. Cover and cook over low heat for 10 minutes. Taste and add salt and pepper, if necessary. Serve hot or cold. Makes about 2 cups.

Time: 20 minutes, excluding time for cooking the artichokes
Servings: 4
Calories: 115 per serving

Note: *To cook artichokes, first cut the stem off flush with the bottom of the artichoke. Then break off the tough outer leaves of the artichoke (one or two layers will do). Turn the artichoke upside down on a flat surface and press on the

---

*If you cannot find fresh artichokes or don't have the time to prepare them, as mentioned, canned or jarred artichokes can be used when drained and rinsed in cold water.

bottom to spread out the leaves. Drop the prepared artichokes into rapidly boiling salted water and cook over medium heat until a leaf can be pulled off the artichoke easily. Remove from the water and drain upside down.

VEAL LIMONE MANCINI

8   veal scaloppine (about 2 ounces each)
2   tablespoons vegetable oil
2   shallots, peeled
1/2 cup dry white wine
    Pinch of freshly ground black pepper
3   lemons
2   teaspoons chopped fresh Italian parsley leaves

1. Flatten the scaloppine with the flat side of a cleaver to make them thinner.

2. Heat the oil in a large frying pan. Chop the shallots into the pan and add the veal slices. Sauté the veal for 2 minutes on each side.

3. Pour the wine over the veal and sprinkle in the pepper. Cook for 2 minutes.

4. Meanwhile, squeeze 2 of the lemons and cut the third into very thin slices. Remove any seeds from the slices. Add the lemon juice and lemon slices to the veal. Stir well and cook for a few minutes longer, or until heated through. Sprinkle with parsley. Serve immediately or let the dish cool and serve cold.

Time: 10 minutes
Servings: 4
Calories: 325 per serving

DAY TWELVE

VENETIAN FISH STEW

> 2 pounds assorted fish and shellfish, such as sea bass, cod,
>   clams, mussels, shrimps, etc.
> 1 onion (3 ounces), peeled and sliced
> 1 large bay leaf
> 2 sprigs fresh parsley
> 1 pound ripe plum tomatoes
> 3 tablespoons olive oil
> 2 garlic cloves, peeled
> 3 shallots, peeled
> 1 onion (4 ounces), peeled
> 1/4 cup chopped fresh Italian parsley leaves
> 1/4 cup chopped fresh basil leaves
> 1/2 cup dry white wine
> 1/3 teaspoon crumbled dried thyme
> 4 slices whole wheat Italian bread

1. To make the fish stock, dress the fish, saving all heads, bones, and trimmings. Discard the shells from the shellfish.

2. Put heads and trimmings into a large kettle and cover with 6 cups of water. Add 1/2 tablespoon of salt. Toss in the onion slices, bay leaf, and parsley sprigs. Bring to a boil and simmer for 1 hour.

3. Strain the stock through a coarse sieve; then strain again through a fine sieve lined with cheesecloth. There should be about 3 cups of strained stock. Set aside.

4. When the stock has been strained, wash tomatoes and cut out the cores. Chop the tomatoes. There should be about 2 cups.

5. Cut the boneless dressed fish into 1-inch pieces. Large shrimp can be split.

6. Heat the oil in a deep saucepan and push the garlic through a press into the oil. Chop the shallots and onion into the pan. Sauté until the onion is translucent.

7. Add fish pieces, parsley, and basil to the pan and brown fish on both sides. Pour in the wine, 3 cups of the fish stock, the tomatoes, and thyme. Simmer for 10 minutes.

8. While stew is simmering, toast the bread slices until they are quite hard, or sauté them in 1 tablespoon of olive oil. Serve the stew with the toasted bread slices.

Time: Stock—1 1/4 hours; Stew—25 minutes

Servings: 4

Calories: 300 per serving (based on sea bass and shrimp),
           including toast

ARTICHOKE AND MUSHROOM SALAD

    4 *medium-sized fresh artichoke bottoms, cooked and cooled*
       (see Note page 162) (Jarred variety can be used
       if rinsed thoroughly)
    6 *large fresh mushrooms*
1 1/2 *tablespoons vegetable oil*
    2 *tablespoons red wine vinegar*
    1 *tablespoon Dijon mustard*
    1 *teaspoon Italian seasoning*
    8 *perfect lettuce leaves*

1. Discard any leaves and the chokes from the artichoke bottoms. Cut the bottoms into thin slices.

2. Wash and trim the mushrooms and cut them into slices a little thinner than the artichoke slices. Combine the vegetables in a bowl.

3. Mix the oil, vinegar, mustard, and Italian seasoning. Pour the dressing over the vegetables and toss to combine well.

4. Arrange 2 lettuce leaves on each plate and divide the salad among them.

Variation
Decorate with a few black olives or pimiento strips or chopped parsley or mix any of these into the salad.

Time: 10 minutes, excluding time to cook and
              cool the artichokes
Servings: 4
Calories: 90 per serving

LINGUINE WITH CHICKEN SAUCE

1 pound linguine or fettucine
2 boneless and skinless chicken breast halves (5 ounces each)
2 tablespoons sweet (unsalted) butter
4 shallots, peeled and minced
3 tablespoons chopped fresh Italian parsley leaves
1/4 teaspoon Italian seasoning
1/4 cup dry white wine

1. Fill a large pot with cold water. Bring to a boil over high heat. Add salt, if desired. Then add the pasta and cook, stirring occasionally, just until the pasta is *al dente*. Drain the pasta in a colander.

2. Flatten the chicken breasts and chop them into small pieces.

3. Melt the butter in a large frying pan and add shallots and part of the parsley. Sauté for a few minutes; then add the chicken and Italian seasoning and toss until it is slightly browned.

4. Add the wine, cover the pan, and cook for a few minutes longer. Stir, then add pepper to taste, and the remaining parsley. Cook for 5 minutes.

5. Add the drained pasta to the sauce in the pan. Mix sauce and pasta quickly then let everything cook together for few minutes. (This is the "Segretto" method.) Serve at once, with Parmesan cheese if you like.

Variation

Add mushrooms, green peppers, or 1 cup diced tomatoes instead of the wine sauce.

Time: 15 to 20 minutes
Servings: 8
Calories: 325 per serving of pasta and sauce

GRAPEFRUIT AND BANANA ICE

  1 cup puréed fresh grapefruit and banana, mixed half and half
1/4 cup fresh lemon juice
  3 tablespoons brandy

  1. Combine the fruit purée, lemon juice, and brandy in a large metal bowl.
  2. Set the bowl in a larger container filled with crushed ice. Stir the mixture with a large wire whisk until it is smooth and creamy. (It is never actually frozen.) Serve immediately.

Time: 20 minutes
Servings: 4
Calories: 90 per serving

DAY THIRTEEN

VEGETABLE SALAD ISCHIA

    2   potatoes (3 ounces each)
1 1/2   pounds fresh broccoli
  3/4   pound fresh string beans
    4   zucchini (4 ounces each)
  1/2   pound ripe plum tomatoes
  1/2   cup chopped celery
  1/2   cup chopped scallions
  1/4   cup chopped fresh Italian parsley leaves
    1   tablespoon minced fresh basil leaves
    3   tablespoons red wine vinegar
    3   tablespoons vegetable oil
    1   tablespoon Dijon mustard

1. Scrub the potatoes and put them in a saucepan. Cover the potatoes with cold water, cover the pan, and boil for 15 minutes, or until the potatoes are tender. Drain and cool.

2. While the potatoes are cooking, blanch broccoli and string beans. Cut off the broccoli flowerets. (Use stems for another recipe.) Wash the beans, top and tail them, and cut them into 1-inch slices. In separate pans, cover the broccoli and beans with cold water, bring to a boil, and simmer for 5 minutes. Drain and cool.

3. Scrub and trim zucchini and cut into thin round slices.

4. Wash the tomatoes and cut out the cores. Dice the tomatoes.

5. Peel the cooked potatoes and cut them into thin slices.

6. Put all the vegetables into a large bowl and add the celery, scallions, and herbs.

7. Mix the vinegar, oil, and mustard together. Pour the dressing over the vegetables and toss gently to mix. Cover and chill until ready to serve.

Time: 20 minutes, excluding the time for chilling
Servings: 8
Calories: 90 per serving

ISH SOUP ABRUZZI STYLE

    2 pounds dressed fresh fish, such as cod, halibut, sea bass, or
      shellfish, weighed after dressing
1/2 pound ripe plum tomatoes
  to 8 shallots
    3 tablespoons olive oil
    1 garlic clove, peeled
1/4 cup chopped fresh Italian parsley leaves
1/3 teaspoon Italian seasoning
    1 cup water
    3 tablespoons white wine vinegar

1. Cut the fish into small pieces.

2. Wash the tomatoes and remove the cores. Chop the omatoes. There should be about 1 cup.

3. Peel and chop shallots. There should be about 1/3 up.

4. Heat the olive oil in a 3-quart pot and push the garlic hrough a press into the hot oil. Add the chopped shallots nd half of the parsley. Sauté until the shallots are ranslucent.

5. Add the tomatoes and cook for 2 or 3 minutes. Then dd the Italian seasoning, water, and fish. Cover the pot and ook for 5 minutes.

6. Add the vinegar but do not cover the pot again. Cook apidly for a few minutes until the liquid is reduced. Stir in he remaining parsley.

Time: 25 minutes
Servings: 6
Calories: 195 per serving

SPAGHETTI WITH EGGPLANT SAUCE SALA

5   small eggplants, or 1 medium-sized eggplant
    (about 1 pound)
2   tablespoons olive oil
2   garlic cloves, crushed
3   shallots, or 1/4 cup diced yellow onion
1/4 teaspoon crushed hot red pepper flakes
2   cups canned imported Italian plum tomatoes with juice,
    coarsely chopped
1/4 cup chopped fresh Italian parsley leaves
1   pound green fettucine or linguine
3   tablespoons freshly grated Parmesan cheese, approximately

1. Peel and slice the eggplant and soak it in salted cold water for 15 minutes. Then rinse and dry it.

2. Put the oil, garlic, shallots, crushed red pepper, and diced eggplant in a large frying pan. Sauté, stirring often, for 8 to 10 minutes.

3. Add the tomatoes and parsley and cook for another 10 to 15 minutes.

4. Meanwhile, fill a large pot with cold water. Bring to a boil over high heat. Then add the pasta and cook, stirring occasionally, just until the pasta is *al dente.* Drain the pasta in a colander.

5. Pour some of the sauce into a warmed serving bowl and add the pasta. Sprinkle with the Parmesan cheese and toss. Add the rest of the sauce and toss again. Serve immediately.

Variation

Add 1/2 cup sliced fresh mushrooms and sauté with the shallots. The sauce can be made without the tomatoes, using just the eggplant, shallots, garlic, and mushroom mixture with lots of parsley.

Time: 25 minutes
Servings: 6
Calories: 270 per serving

MUSHROOM SALAD

For this dish, use only perfect unblemished white mushrooms.

    6 large fresh mushrooms
    1 tablespoon olive oil
    1 tablespoon white wine vinegar
    1 tablespoon Dijon mustard
    2 perfect Bibb lettuce leaves
    2 teaspoons snipped fresh chives

1. Wash the mushrooms, but do not peel them. Cut off the stem ends of the mushrooms. Cut through the cap and stem to make very thin slices. Put the mushroom slices in a bowl.

2. Mix together the olive oil, vinegar, and mustard. Season with black pepper to taste. Pour the dressing over the raw mushroom slices until they are well coated. Spoon the mushrooms onto the lettuce leaves on 2 plates and sprinkle the chives over the mushrooms.

Variation

Add 3 medium-sized chopped cooked shrimp and toss.

Time: 5 minutes
Servings: 2
Calories: 87 per serving

BRAISED LAMB IN WINE SAUCE

> 2 *pounds boneless lamb cut into 1/4-inch cubes,*
>   *from the shoulder or leg*
> 1 *tablespoon vegetable oil*
> 3 *shallots, peeled*
> 1 *garlic clove, peeled*
> 3 *tablespoons minced fresh Italian parsley leaves*
> 1/2 *cup dry red wine*
> 1 *tablespoon Italian seasoning*

1. Cut all fat off the lamb and flatten the cubes with the flat side of a cleaver to make them into thin pieces.

2. Heat the oil in a large frying pan with a cover. Chop the shallots into the pan and push the garlic through a press into the pan. Add the parsley and the flattened pieces of lamb. Sauté over brisk heat until lamb pieces are lightly browned on both sides.

3. Add the wine and Italian seasoning and bring to a boil over high heat. Reduce the heat until the liquid in the pan is barely simmering. Cover the pan and braise for 8 to 10 minutes, or until the lamb is tender and done to your taste. Taste for seasoning and add more Italian seasoning, if necessary, and black pepper to taste before serving.

Time: 20 minutes
Servings: 6
Calories: 350 per serving

STRAWBERRY FLUFF AMARETTO

    3 egg whites at room temperature
    1/4 teaspoon cream of tartar
    1/4 teaspoon vanilla extract
    2 teaspoons fresh lemon juice
    1 tablespoon Amaretto
    2 cups diced hulled strawberries

Beat the egg whites and cream of tartar together with a rotary egg beater or with an electric mixer at high speed, until soft peaks form. Add the vanilla, lemon juice, and Amaretto and continue beating until stiff. At low speed, beat in the diced strawberries. Cover and chill.

Variation

Top the fluff with more strawberries or fresh raspberries or blueberries. Or arrange the berries in a ring around a serving of fluff and top with a fresh mint leaf.

Time: 15 minutes, excluding time for chilling
Servings: 6
Calories: 35 per serving

DAY FOURTEEN

STUFFED EGGPLANT NOUSHA

    1 1-pound eggplant
    1 tablespoon vegetable oil
    3 shallots, peeled
    1 garlic clove, peeled
    3 sprigs fresh Italian parsley, leaves only
    6 fresh mushrooms, washed and trimmed
    1 tablespoon Italian seasoning
       Freshly ground black pepper

1. Wash the eggplant and trim the ends, but do not peel it. Put the whole eggplant into a large pot of boiling water and cook for 6 minutes, or until it is tender. Remove the eggplant from the water and cool for a few minutes. Halve the eggplant lengthwise and scoop out the pulp from each half and chop without damaging the skins.
2. Preheat the oven to 350 degrees.
3. Heat the oil in a large frying pan. Chop the shallots, garlic, and parsley into the pan. Slice the mushrooms very thin and add them to the pan with the Italian seasoning and a pinch of pepper. Sauté for 3 to 4 minutes. Add the eggplant pulp and mix well.
4. Stuff the eggplant shells with the mixture. Bake for 10 minutes.

Variations
Sprinkle the stuffed eggplants with grated Parmesan, mozzarella, or ricotta.
While sautéing the filling mixture, add 1 cup crushed, canned tomatoes or 1 cup ricotta mixed with 1 lightly beaten egg.

Time: 20 minutes
Servings: 4
Calories: 50 per serving

SHRIMP IN GARLIC SAUCE

>   2 *pounds raw jumbo shrimp in the shells*
>   3 *tablespoons vegetable oil*
>   3 *garlic cloves, peeled*
>   2 *shallots, peeled*
> 1/4 *cup dry white wine*
>   *Juice of 1 lemon*
> 1/4 *cup chopped fresh Italian parsley leaves*

1. Shell and devein the shrimp. Rinse them in cold water and pat them dry.
2. Heat the oil in a large frying pan. Push the garlic through a press into the oil. Mince the shallots into the oil as well. Sauté for 1 or 2 minutes.
3. Add the shrimp and toss in the oil. Add the wine, lemon juice, and parsley and cook for a few minutes longer.
4. Serve hot over rice.

Time: 20 minutes
Servings: 4
Calories: 238 per serving (excluding the rice)

FRUIT PURÉE

Portions of fruit purée can be served as a side dish in place of a vegetable. Fruits to use are apples, apricots, bananas, cherries, oranges, pineapple, raspberries, and strawberries.

These purées make excellent sauces for main courses and desserts. Use your imagination to combine two or more fruits for unusual different tastes.

    1   cup diced fresh fruit or whole ripe berries
    1/2 cup part skim ricotta or lowfat cottage cheese

Prepare the fresh fruit by peeling or removing the pits or seeds or cores, as necessary. Chop the fruit and put it in a blender container. Add the ricotta or cottage cheese and blend to a purée.

Variation

When preparing these for desserts or dessert sauces, add 2 to 3 tablespoons of Marsala or Grand Marnier when adding the cheese.

Time: 10 minutes

Servings: 4

Calories: 60 to 80, depending on the fruit used

VEAL CHOPS SALA

    3   tablespoons olive oil
    6   shallots, diced
    2   garlic cloves, crushed
  1/4   cup chopped fresh Italian parsley leaves
    6   veal loin chops (5 ounces each)
  1/2   cup dry red wine
    4   large artichoke bottoms, cooked and diced
        (see Note page 162)
    1   cup finely sliced fresh mushrooms
        Freshly ground black pepper

1. Heat the oil in a large frying pan and add the diced shallots, parsley, and garlic. Sauté for a few minutes, stirring often.

2. Add the veal chops and sauté for 2 to 3 minutes on each side. (Slash the top to see if the chop goes from pink to white.) Do not overcook.

3. Add the wine, diced artichokes, and mushrooms and cook for 5 minutes longer. Add parsley and cook for 2 more minutes. Sprinkle with freshly ground black pepper and serve immediately.

Time: 15 minutes, excluding time to cook and
           cool the artichokes
Servings: 6
Calories: 275 per serving

10-POUND 30-DAY MAINTENANCE PLAN

You're at your desired weight, thanks to the Pasta Diet, and you can again fit into those clothes you had sadly "outgrown." But now begins the long haul, because you want to keep your new figure. The recipes in this maintenance section will help you do just that.

The maintenance recipes give you more freedom than the 14-day plan. But with freedom comes responsibility. I've selected the maintenance recipes to allow you either to continue losing weight gradually or simply to maintain it at the desired level.

The following section enables you to construct your own menu program based on your particular goals. If you wish to shed more pounds, use the maintenance recipes and guidelines of the Pasta Diet to pace your own weight loss.

For example, in order to lose ten pounds a month, construct menus ranging approximately between 1,200 and 1,800 calories a day. (If you splurge one day on 1,800 calories, use a 1,200-calorie plan the next day.) To lose five pounds a month stay between 1,500 and 2,200 calories a day. To simply maintain your weight, stick to approximately 2,500 calories a day. (Again, if you splurge on the 2,500-calorie plan, pick a recipe from the 14-day program the next day to make up for your indulgence.)

While maintaining your weight you must learn to deal with snacking. Those who have followed my pasta way-of-eating now snack the Italian way, that is, using raw vegetables, such as carrots or celery, and dipping them into the sauces suggested by my Pasta Diet, or fresh fruit.

I also recommend that you keep a record of your calorie intake. From my experience with weight loss, I've learned that it's best to keep track of the calories you consume until the maintenance pattern has become routine. The calorie record will ensure that if you do go to excess, you can correct the matter by employing some of the low-calorie treats of the Pasta Diet. You will get to the point where you can look at food and portions and approximate the calorie count.

STOCKS

Homemade stock takes time to prepare, but, when it is completed, it can be stored in refrigerator or freezer, ready for use in soups and sauces. Your own stock can be as flavorful as you like, and as lightly salted as you like, an advantage over most commercial stocks. Meat stocks need long cooking, but a useful vegetable stock can be ready in 30 minutes.

CHICKEN STOCK ITALIAN STYLE

My mother's secret for superior chicken stock was to add a small chunk (about 1 1/2 ounces) of Parmesan or Pecorino cheese to the chicken stock while it was cooking.

    4 pounds chicken parts (bones, necks, backs, and wings)
    3 leeks
    3 celery stalks
    1 ripe tomato (5 ounces)
    1 carrot
    1 white onion (1 ounce)
    2 teaspoons crushed black peppercorns
    5 sprigs fresh Italian parsley
    1 teaspoon fresh or dried thyme
    1 bay leaf
  1/4 teaspoon Italian seasoning

1. Rinse the chicken parts well and put them into a large stockpot.

2. Wash, scrape, or peel the vegetables, and chop them into the stockpot. Add the crushed peppercorns, herbs, and Italian seasoning. Pour in enough water to reach 1 inch above the ingredients.

3. Cover the pot and bring to boil. Lower the heat and simmer for about 2 hours.

4. Use a fork to remove the chicken pieces and discard. Strain everything else in the stockpot through a sieve lined with dampened cheesecloth into a bowl. Chill the stock.

5. When the stock is cold, lift off the fat that has risen to the surface. Transfer the stock into jars for refrigerator storage, or pour into 1-cup containers or into an ice-cube tray for freezer storage. When completely frozen, the cubes can be transferred to a plastic freezer bag. Use the cubes a few at a time, as you need them.

Time: 2 hours
Servings: Makes about 2 quarts
Calories: 30 per cup

VEAL STOCK

3 *pounds meaty veal bones (shanks or knuckles)*
1 *onion (4 ounces)*
2 *whole cloves*
1 *large carrot*
1/2 *cup chopped fresh Italian parsley stems*
1 *bay leaf*
2 *coriander seeds, crushed*
1/2 *pound boneless veal from the breast, shoulder, or flank*
1/2 *teaspoon Italian seasoning*

1. Put the veal bones in a large stockpot (8 quarts is the ideal size). Cover with cold water, bring to a boil, and boil for 5 minutes, skimming often. Pour off the water and rinse the veal bones and the pot.

2. Return the bones to the pot and pour in 4 quarts of cold water.

3. Peel the onion and stick the cloves into it. Add the onion to the stockpot.

4. Wash and scrape the carrot and cut it into chunks. Add the carrot chunks to the stockpot along with the parsley stems, bay leaf, and coriander. Bring to a boil; then lower the heat to a simmer. Half-cover the pot and cook for 5 to 6 hours. During the first hour skim the stock often. After 4 hours, add the boneless veal and Italian seasoning.

5. Taste the stock after 5 hours. It should be flavorful; if not, cook for 1 hour longer. Let the stock stand for 10 minutes, then ladle it through a coarse strainer. All vegetables and herbs will be flavorless, so discard them. The boneless veal and any scraps of meat from the bones can be saved for stuffing vegetables.

6. Pour the stock through a fine strainer lined with dampened cheesecloth into a bowl. Chill the stock. Discard any fat that has risen to the top. The stock will keep in the refrigerator for at least 5 days, or it can be frozen in 1-cup containers or ice-cube trays.

Time: 6 hours
Servings: Makes about 2 quarts
Calories: 35 per cup

VEGETABLE STOCK

    4 cups water
    1 cup chopped vegetables (see Note)
    2 tablespoons chopped fresh Italian parsley leaves
    1/2 teaspoon minced fresh basil leaves
    1/4 teaspoon Italian seasoning

Combine all the ingredients in a saucepan. Cover the pan and bring to a boil. Lower the heat to simmer and cook for 30 minutes. Strain the sauce through a cheesecloth-lined sieve into a bowl. Freeze in 1-cup containers or in ice-cube trays.

Note: Use 2 or 3 kinds of vegetables, according to the season. Choose from carrots, leeks, onions, potatoes, tomatoes, or zucchini. Wash, peel if necessary, and cut into small pieces.

Time: 30 minutes
Servings: Makes about 4 cups clear soup
Calories: 10 per cup

DIPS AND SAUCES

VEGETABLE PURÉES

Purées can be used as a vegetable accompaniment or as a salad ingredient. They are also useful for appetizers. Use as a dip or dressing or to stuff other vegetables. To use as a sauce, thin to the correct texture with wine or stock.

 2 cups vegetables cut into small pieces
 1 cup part skim ricotta or lowfat cottage cheese
 2 shallots, peeled and minced
1/2 to 1 teaspoon herbs and/or spices of your choice

1. Steam the vegetables until they are tender. Drain them if necessary.
2. Put the vegetables in a blender container with the cheese. Add the minced shallots and herbs and/or spices. Blend to a purée.

Time: 15 minutes
Servings: 4
Calories: 60 per 1/2 cup

EGGPLANT DIP

 3 shallots, peeled
 3 sprigs fresh Italian parsley
 4 medium-sized ripe tomatoes
 2 medium-sized eggplants (about 1 pound each)
 1 tablespoon vegetable oil
 2 garlic cloves, peeled
 1 tablespoon Italian seasoning
   Pinch of cayenne pepper

1. Dice the shallots.
2. Use kitchen scissors to snip parsley, including the stems, into bits.
3. Bring a saucepan of water to a boil. Remove the cores from the tomatoes and drop the tomatoes into the boiling water. Remove from the heat and let the tomatoes sit in the water for 2 to 3 minutes. Then transfer them to a bowl of

cold water and let them sit in the cold water for 2 to 3 minutes, or until the skins begin to pucker. Peel the tomatoes and squeeze out the seeds. Chop the tomatoes into small pieces.

4. Peel the eggplants last (lest they discolor).

5. Heat the oil in a large frying pan over high heat and dice the peeled eggplant into the oil. Add the shallots, and push the garlic through a press into the mixture. Mix well.

6. Lower heat to medium and cook for 3 minutes.

7. Add the snipped parsley, chopped tomatoes, Italian seasoning, and cayenne pepper to taste. Continue to cook for 8 to 10 minutes, but you can cook it a little longer if you prefer a softer texture. Makes 5 cups.

Variations

Instead of eggplant, use the same weight of zucchini. If fresh from the garden, don't peel them. If they are market vegetables with tougher skins, scrape with a vegetable peeler, taking off the thinnest possible layer of skin. With either eggplant or zucchini, add chopped or sliced olives.

Use chopped red peppers.

If fresh tomatoes are not available, use 2 cups canned imported Italian tomatoes.

Omit tomatoes and instead use 2 cups of dry red wine.

Instead of peeling the eggplants, leave the purple skin on the pieces. It will add quite a different taste and color to the finished sauce.

For a smooth sauce, purée the mixture in a blender or through a food mill. The food mill will remove the tomato and eggplant seeds, making the sauce easier to digest. Reheat the sauce to serve.

Time: 20 minutes
Servings: 16 (5 tablespoons each)
Calories: 25 per 5 tablespoons

EMILIO'S ARTICHOKE SAUCE
(For Pasta)

6 *fresh baby artichokes*
1/3 *cup virgin olive oil*
4 *fresh red tomatoes*
4 *cloves garlic*
1 *tablespoon fresh parsley*
1/4 *cup grated pecorino cheese*
Pepper to taste

1. Cut away the leaves of the artichokes and use only the centers (hearts). Cut the hearts into small pieces.
2. Chop the parsley; crush the garlic; dice the tomatoes.
3. Heat the oil in a saucepan and saute the garlic for a couple of minutes. Add the artichokes, parsley, and tomatoes and cook six to eight minutes, covered, stirring often. Serve over cooked rigatoni or penne pasta and top with pecorino cheese.

Time: 15 minutes
Servings: 6 servings
Calories: 230

TOMATO-CURRY DIP

1 cup tomato sauce (below)
1 tablespoon Dijon mustard
1 tablespoon curry powder
2 tablespoons snipped fresh dill

Put all the ingredients into a blender container and process until smooth. Cover and chill.

Time: 5 minutes, excluding time for chilling
Servings: makes 1 1/4 cups
Calories: 4 per tablespoon

BASIC TOMATO SAUCE

1   medium white onion
1   clove garlic
2   fresh basil leaves
1   cup fresh plum tomatoes or canned imported Italian plum
     tomatoes
1   tablespoon extra virgin olive oil
1/2 teaspoon Italian seasoning
     Pinch of cayenne pepper

1. Chop the onion very fine; crush the garlic and chop the basil leaves. Dice the tomatoes. 2. Add the oil to a large frying pan. Add the onions, garlic, and seasoning, and sauté a few minutes. Add the tomatoes. (Be sure to drain the liquid of the canned tomatoes.) Cook the sauce 5 to 8 minutes and add the basil leaves and cayenne pepper at the last minute.

Time: 10 minutes
Servings: 4 (3 tablespoons per serving)
Calories: 30 per tablespoon

SIMPLE PESTO
(For Pasta, Fish, and Eggs)

For the perfect taste of this simple sauce with so few ingredients, use only the finest quality ingredients. Use no garlic or salt or pepper.

   2 cups large fresh basil leaves without stems
   3 tablespoons freshly grated Romano cheese
   3 tablespoons olive oil
1/4 cup chopped fresh Italian parsley leaves

1. Wash the basil leaves thoroughly in cold water; then dry them.

2. Put the basil in a blender container with the cheese, oil, and parsley. Blend for 5 seconds, or until smooth and creamy. Stop the machine and stir with a spoon at intervals.

3. Refrigerate the pasta to serve it cold, or warm it for a few minutes to serve it hot. Cover with a thin film of oil, or press a sheet of plastic film tightly over the surface if you are going to store the pesto, or it will turn black. If too dry, add a few tablespoons of hot water.

Variations

For a creamy texture add 3 tablespoons of ricotta.

If good Romano cheese is not available, use Parmesan. Add a dash of lemon.

Time: 5 minutes
Servings: 5 or 6—makes 1 cup (3 tablespoons each)
Calories: 50 per tablespoon

ELISA'S PESTO WITH SPINACH

*It isn't easy to find fresh basil during the winter and early spring.
Frozen basil can be used. This recipe was devised for the times when
basil is scarce and you can find only a little.*

    3   cups fresh spinach leaves without stems, washed and drained
    1   cup chopped fresh Italian parsley leaves
    1/2 cup fresh basil leaves without stems
    2   garlic cloves, peeled
    1/4 cup olive oil
    1/4 cup freshly grated Parmesan cheese
    6   tablespoons hot water

Put the spinach, parsley, and basil in a blender
container. Push the garlic through a press into the mixture
and add the oil and cheese. Process until the sauce is
smooth. Mix in the hot water. (Use the water from cooking
the pasta if you are preparing this to serve with pasta.)

Note: This sauce has many other uses. It can be used with
vegetables, soups, eggs, and pasta salads.

Time: 10 minutes
Servings: About 10 (1/4 cup each)
Calories: 110 per 1/4 cup

RICOTTA-EGG DIP OR SAUCE

1/2   cup part skim ricotta
2   hard-boiled egg yolks
2   tablespoons snipped fresh dill or dill weed
1   tablespoon Dijon mustard
    Pinch of cayenne pepper

Put all the ingredients except the cayenne in a blender container and process until smooth. Cover and chill. Add a zesty taste by adding a pinch of cayenne pepper just before serving. Use for vegetables, seafood, poultry or meats—even pasta. Serve hot or cold.

Time: 5 minutes, excluding time for chilling
Servings: Makes about 1 cup
Calories: 13 per tablespoon

VINAIGRETTE DRESSING

2   tablespoons extra virgin olive oil
2   tablespoons red wine vinegar
1/2   tablespoon Dijon mustard
1   tablespoon snipped fresh dill
1/4   teaspoon Italian seasoning
2   shallots, peeled and minced

The ingredients can all be mixed together, but a better way to dress a salad is to pour the oil into the greens first and toss well. Then mix the remaining ingredients together and pour them over the salad. Toss again. Makes about 6 tablespoons.

Time: 5 minutes
Servings: 4 (1 1/2 tablespoons each)
Calories: 23 per tablespoon

CAPER DRESSING
(For Salad, Fish, Veal, Cold Vegetables, and Pasta Salads)

    2 hard-boiled eggs, shelled
    1/4 cup red wine vinegar
    3 tablespoons extra virgin olive oil
    2 tablespoons drained chopped capers
    1 garlic clove, peeled and crushed
       Pinch of cayenne pepper

Mash the eggs and put them in a blender container with all the other ingredients. Blend for 2 seconds, or until well mixed and smooth. Cover and chill. Makes about 1 1/2 cups.

Time: 5 minutes
Servings: 8 (3 tablespoons each)
Calories: 65 per 3 tablespoons

PEPPER AND ONION DRESSING

    1/2 cup red wine vinegar
    3 tablespoons vegetable oil
    1/4 teaspoon paprika
    3 tablespoons chopped shallots
    1 garlic clove, crushed
    3 tablespoons chopped sweet green pepper
    2 tablespoons chopped fresh Italian parsley leaves
    2 tablespoons chopped fresh dill
    3 tablespoons Dijon mustard
    1/2 teaspoon cayenne pepper

Mix all the ingredients together in a bowl or bottle. Cover and chill. Serve over a variety of mixed greens or vegetables. Makes about 1 1/2 cups.

Time: 6 minutes
Servings: 8 (3 tablespoons each)
Calories: 45 per 3 tablespoons

SALSA VERDE
(Green Sauce for Seafood, Boiled Meat, Eggs, Pasta, and Pasta Salads)

1/2	cup chopped fresh Italian parsley leaves
1/4	cup chopped shallots
3	tablespoons chopped fresh basil leaves
3	tablespoons snipped fresh chives
2	garlic cloves, crushed and peeled
1	teaspoon chopped fresh tarragon
3	tablespoons olive oil
1/4	cup red wine vinegar
	Juice of 1/2 lemon
1 1/2	tablespoons Dijon mustard
1	hard-boiled egg, mashed

Combine all the ingredients except the egg together in a large bowl. Mix well. Put in a blender container and whirl for a few seconds. (Do not overblend, as the sauce needs texture.) Add the egg and blend for another second. Cover and chill or serve at room temperature. Makes about 1 3/4 cups.

Time: 10 minutes, excluding chilling time
Servings: 10 (3 tablespoons each)
Calories: 50 per 3 tablespoons

VEGETABLES

BRAISED ARTICHOKES WITH TOMATOES

    4 cooked artichoke bottoms (see Note page 162)
    8 large ripe plum tomatoes
    1 teaspoon vegetable oil
       Juice of 1 1/2 lemons
    2 teaspoons grated lemon rind
    4 shallots, peeled and minced
    4 teaspoons minced fresh Italian parsley leaves

1. Remove the leaves from the artichokes and scoop out the chokes. Cut the bottoms from top to bottom into halves, to make half-moons.

2. Bring a saucepan of water to a boil. Remove the cores from the tomatoes and drop the tomatoes into the boiling water. Remove from the heat and let the tomatoes sit in the water for 2 to 3 minutes. Then transfer them to a bowl of cold water and let them sit in the cold water for 2 to 3 minutes, or until the skins begin to pucker. Peel the tomatoes carefully. Over a strainer set in a bowl, carefully slit each tomato lengthwise and scoop out the interior, including the seeds and juice.

3. Set the rounded side of each artichoke piece into the slit in one of the tomatoes.

4. Using 1/2 teaspoon of the oil or less, oil the bottom and sides of a 6-cup baking dish or any baking dish with a diameter of about 7 inches. Arrange the packages of artichoke and tomato around the dish in a single layer; they should just fit.

5. Mix the tomato juice that has drained through the strainer with the lemon juice, and measure. There should be at least 1/2 cup. If there is less, add enough water to make up the difference. Pour the mixture over the artichokes. Mix the lemon rind, shallots, and parsley together and scatter the mixture evenly over the top.

6. Preheat the oven to 350 degrees.

7. With the remaining oil, coat a sheet of foil, and press it, oiled side down, over the vegetables. Make a tiny hole in the center of the foil for steam to escape, and cover the baking dish tightly with the foil.

8. Bake for 20 minutes. Lift off the foil without letting any condensed steam fall into the vegetables and serve from the baking dish.

Time: 30 minutes, excluding time for
           cooking the artichokes
Servings: 4
Calories: 65 per serving

VEGETABLE CASSEROLE ROMA

    1 pound mixed vegetables, such as eggplant, potatoes,
       tomatoes, and zucchini
    2 eggs
    1 cup dried bread crumbs, made from whole wheat Italian
       bread
  1/2 cup chopped fresh Italian parsley leaves
  1/4 cup shallots
    3 tablespoons chopped fresh basil leaves
  1/3 teaspoon Italian seasoning
    1 garlic clove, peeled
    1 tablespoon olive oil
    1 cup diced or shredded part skim mozzarella

1. Wash and trim the vegetables and peel them if necessary. Cut all the vegetables into thin slices.

2. Break the eggs into a bowl and beat until well mixed but not foamy. Stir in the bread crumbs, parsley, shallots, basil, and Italian seasoning. Push the garlic through a press into the mixture and mix thoroughly.

3. Preheat the oven to 350 degrees. Use the oil to coat a 9-inch-deep pie dish or a 6-cup square or rectangular pan.

4. Layer some of the vegetables in the oiled pan, and then spoon part of the crumb mixture over. Sprinkle with part of the mozzarella. Continue making layers of vegetables, seasonings, crumb mixture, and cheese. If there is enough, make a third layer. The top layer should be of cheese.

5. Bake for 20 minutes. If you used a round pan, cut into wedges to serve. A rectangular casserole can be cut into squares.

Time: 30 minutes
Servings: 6
Calories: 125 per serving

TOMATOES STUFFED WITH EGGPLANT

    16 firm medium-sized tomatoes
     2 cloves garlic
     1 1-pound eggplant
     2 tablespoons extra virgin olive oil
     3 tablespoons fresh lemon juice
     1 tablespoon drained capers
     2 tablespoons minced fresh Italian parsley leaves
     1 tablespoon snipped fresh chives
        Pinch of cayenne pepper
    16 tiny parsley sprigs or watercress sprigs

1. Wash the tomatoes and cut off a thin slice at the stem end of each tomato. Scoop out the insides without damaging the shells. (Use the scooped-out portions for tomato sauce or juice.) Drain the tomatoes upside down. Crush the garlic.

2. Peel the eggplant and cut the flesh into chunks. Steam the eggplant chunks over 1 cup of water until tender. Turn into a food mill and purée. (This is the best method, as it removes all the seeds and any stringy portions.) There

should be about 1 cup of purée. Let it cool, then stir in the olive oil, lemon juice, garlic, cayenne pepper, capers, parsley, and chives.

3. Spoon enough of the purée into each tomato to fill. Top with a parsley or watercress sprig, and serve cold.

Variations

Omit the capers and chives.

Sprinkle the tops of the stuffed tomatoes with grated Parmesan cheese and bake in a preheated 375-degree oven for 15 minutes.

Time: 15 minutes
Servings: 8 (2 tomatoes per serving)
Calories: 21 per tomato

EGGPLANT DIO

    3 tablespoons vegetable oil
    1 cup uncooked natural brown rice
2 1/2 cups water
       Salt
    1 1-pound eggplant
    2 zucchini (6 ounces each)
    2 sweet green peppers
    3 shallots
    2 garlic cloves, peeled
  1/4 cup chopped fresh Italian parsley leaves
    1 tablespoon grated fresh gingerroot
  1/2 teaspoon cayenne pepper
    1 cup part skim ricotta, or 4 ounces (1 cup) shredded part
       skim mozzarella

1. Heat 1 tablespoon of the oil in a saucepan with a tight-fitting cover. Add the rice and stir to coat every grain with oil. Add 1/2 cup water, cover, and let the rice cook until

the liquid has been absorbed. Add another 1/2 cup of water and again cook until the water has been absorbed. Continue adding water until the rice is cooked *al dente*. If the rice is cooked to your taste with less water, do not use it at all. Turn the cooked rice into an 8-cup casserole.

2. While the rice is cooking, wash and trim the eggplant, but do not peel it. Cut the eggplant into small cubes and immediately drop the cubes into a saucepan of water with a pinch of salt. Simmer for a few minutes, or until the eggplant is tender. Drain.

3. Wash and trim the zucchini. Peel them and cut them into small cubes.

4. Wash and trim the green peppers, discarding the ribs and seeds. Chop the peppers.

5. Peel and chop the shallots.

6. Preheat the oven to 350 degrees.

7. Heat the remaining 2 tablespoons of oil in a large frying pan and push the garlic through a press into the hot oil. Add the shallots, green peppers, and zucchini. Sauté until the shallots are translucent. Add the parsley, gingerroot, and cayenne and sauté for 1 minute. Add the drained eggplant cubes and cook for a few minutes, stirring constantly with a wooden spoon to blend all the ingredients.

8. Spoon the vegetable mixture on top of the rice, and sprinkle the cheese over everything. Bake for 10 minutes, or until the ingredients are heated through.

Variations

If the basic recipe is too "hot" for you, use less gingerroot and cayenne.

Cook the rice with chicken stock (more calories) or use 1/4 cup dry Marsala or dry white wine in place of part of the water or stock.

Time: 30 minutes

Servings: 4

Calories: 230 per serving with ricotta; 250 with mozzarella

EGGPLANT CAPONATA

1 1 1/4-pound eggplant
   Salt
2 large sweet green peppers
2 onions (4 ounces each)
1/2 pound ripe plum tomatoes
3 tablespoons extra virgin olive oil
2 garlic cloves, peeled
1 tablespoon red wine vinegar
3 tablespoons drained capers
1/3 teaspoon Italian seasoning
   Pinch of cayenne pepper
1/3 cup chopped fresh Italian parsley leaves

1. Wash and trim the eggplant, but do not peel it. Cut the eggplant into small cubes. There should be about 2 cups. Soak the cubes in cold water with 1 tablespoon salt for each quart of water for 10 minutes. Drain, rinse, drain again, and pat dry.

2. While the eggplant is soaking, wash and trim the peppers, discarding the ribs and seeds. Chop the peppers.

3. Peel and chop the onions.

4. Wash the tomatoes and core them. Chop the tomatoes. There should be 1 cup.

5. Heat the olive oil in a large frying pan and push garlic through a press into the hot oil. Add the onions and sauté until they are translucent. Add the chopped peppers and dried eggplant cubes and sauté, stirring often, for 5 minutes. Add the vinegar, capers, and Italian seasoning and cook for 2 or 3 minutes. Add tomatoes and cook for 5 minutes longer. Taste and add salt and pepper if necessary. Stir in the parsley. Serve warm or cold. Makes 5 to 6 cups.

Time: 20 minutes
Servings: About 10 (1/2 cup each)
Calories: 70 per 1/2 cup

FISH AND SEAFOOD

SHRIMP IN HERB SAUCE

6 to 8 ripe plum tomatoes
    2 pounds raw medium-sized shrimp in the shells
    2 tablespoons vegetable oil
1/4 cup chopped fresh Italian parsley leaves
    1 tablespoon Italian seasoning
    2 tablespoons chopped fresh dill
    1 garlic clove, crushed
        Pinch of cayenne pepper

1. Bring a saucepan of water to a boil. Remove the cores from the tomatoes and drop the tomatoes into the boiling water. Remove from the heat and let the tomatoes sit in the water for 2 to 3 minutes. Then transfer them to a bowl of cold water and let them sit in the cold water for 2 to 3 minutes, or until the skins begin to pucker. Peel the tomatoes and squeeze out the seeds. Chop the tomatoes. There should be about 1 cup.

2. Rinse the shrimp and peel and devein them. Set aside.

3. Pour the oil into a large frying pan and add the tomatoes, parsley, Italian seasoning, dill, cayenne pepper, and garlic. Cook over medium heat for 2 minutes. Season with salt and pepper to taste.

4. Add the shrimp and cook for 6 to 8 minutes, or until the shrimp are pink and tender. Do not overcook and stir often to mix the shrimp into the sauce as they cook. Serve immediately.

Variations

Instead of tomatoes, use 1 cup sautéed chopped mushrooms, green peppers, onions, or zucchini. Or use a mixture of two or more of the vegetables.

Substitute 1/2 cup dry red wine for the tomatoes.

Time: 15 minutes
Servings: 4
Calories: 220 per serving

CALAMARI LUIGI

Buy the smallest squid available. They are the most tender when quickly cooked.

1 1/2 pounds small squid
  1/2 pound ripe plum tomatoes or 1 cup canned imported Italian
       plum tomatoes
    1 medium onion
    1 tablespoon extra virgin olive oil
    2 garlic cloves, peeled
  1/4 cup chopped fresh Italian parsley leaves
  1/4 teaspoon Italian seasoning
       Pinch of cayenne pepper

1. Prepare the squid by removing the mantle, head, and rudimentary shell (like a piece of transparent plastic). With the fingers peel off the purple skin. (It is edible, but it discolors the dish.) Cut the squid into small strips.

2. Wash the tomatoes and remove the cores. Chop the tomatoes. There should be 1 cup.

3. Peel and mince the onion.

4. Heat the oil in a frying pan and push the garlic through a press into the hot oil. Add the onion and half of the parsley and sauté until the onion is translucent. Add the tomatoes, seasonings and simmer for 8 minutes.

5. Squid is edible raw; if it is overcooked, it develops a rubbery texture. Taste a piece and stop cooking the minute it is done. Stir in the rest of the parsley. Serve immediately.

Time: 20 minutes
Servings: 4
Calories: 200

SOLE STUFFED WITH SPINACH

4 sole or flounder fillets, 4 ounces each
1 cup chopped cooked fresh spinach
1/2 cup part skim ricotta
1/2 teaspoon freshly grated nutmeg
1/4 cup chopped fresh Italian parsley leaves
1/2 cup dry white wine
   Juice of 1/2 lemon

1. Preheat the oven to 350 degrees.
2. Spread the fillets out flat. Separate each one at the center seam to make 2 narrow fillets from each one.
3. Mix the spinach, cheese, and nutmeg together in a small bowl. Place 1 tablespoon of the spinach mixture in the center of each strip of fish. Fold one end of the fillet over the filling, then the other end over that, making a three-fold package. Fasten each package with a wooden toothpick or a small skewer.
4. Put the rolls in a baking dish just large enough to hold the rolls in a single layer. Sprinkle the parsley over the rolls. Mix the wine and lemon juice together and spoon the mixture over the rolls, dividing it evenly.
5. Bake for 10 minutes, or until done to your taste. Spoon the wine and lemon juice from the pan over the fish rolls.

Variations
Instead of sole or flounder, this dish can be made with fillets of red snapper or striped bass.

Time: 15 to 20 minutes
Servings: 4 (2 small rolls per person)
Calories: 155 per serving

SAUTÉED FLOUNDER WITH DILL AND WINE SAUCE

4 flounder fillets (4 ounces each)
2 tablespoons vegetable oil
6 shallots, peeled
1/4 cup chopped fresh dill
1/2 cup dry white wine

1. Rinse the fillets and pat them dry. These will be turned over once in cooking. If you have a pancake turner wide enough to slide under the whole fillet, fine. If not, it is better to divide the fillets lengthwise along the natural center division, as the narrow half fillet is easier to turn.

2. Heat the oil in a large frying pan and chop the shallots into the hot oil. Sauté them until they are translucent. Add the dill and heat for 1 minute. Gently lay the fillets in the pan on top of the dill. Sauté for 2 minutes. Carefully but quickly turn the fillets over and cook for 1 minute longer. Add the wine.

3. Serve the fillets at once. Flounder fillets are so thin they will be fully cooked. Scoop out some of the dill and shallots to serve with each fillet; most of the oil should be left in the pan.

Variations

Add chopped garlic.
Use parsley instead of dill.
Sprinkle fresh lemon juice over each fillet when serving.
Other fillets can be prepared this way, but if they are thicker they will need to cook a little longer. Add tomato sauce or mushrooms.

Time: 7 minutes
Servings: 4
Calories: 135 per serving

CODFISH ALLA ADELAIDA

6 pieces boneless fresh cod (4 ounces each)
4 shallots, peeled
2 tablespoons extra virgin olive oil
1/2 cup dry white wine
1/2 cup white raisins
1/4 cup chopped fresh Italian parsley leaves
1/2 cup fresh lemon juice

1. Rinse the codfish pieces and pat them dry.
2. Heat the frying pan. Mince the shallots into the pan with the oil and sauté until they are translucent.
3. Lay pieces of cod in the pan and pour in the wine and raisins. Sprinkle the fish with parsley. Cover the pan and cook for 10 minutes. Decorate with the chopped parsley. Add lemon juice.

Time: 20 minutes
Servings: 6
Calories: 145 per serving

MEATS AND POULTRY

STEAK FLAMBÉ

    4 slices beef sirloin, top round, or eye round (4 ounces each)
    1 tablespoon sweet (unsalted) butter
    1 tablespoon vegetable oil
    3 tablespoons Dijon mustard
  1/2 cup dry red wine
    3 tablespoons Cognac

1. Pound the beef slices flat.

2. Heat the butter and oil in a large frying pan. Add the beef and brown quickly on one side. Turn over, and spread the browned sides of the meat with half the mustard. When the underside is browned, turn over again and spread the second side with the remaining mustard.

3. Pour the wine into the pan and reduce the heat to medium-low. Slash the beef pieces in the center and check for degree of doneness you prefer. Do not overcook the steaks; they are best medium-rare.

4. Heat the Cognac and pour it over the steaks for the last minute of cooking. Ignite the Cognac and let the flame burn out naturally. Serve at once with the sauce spooned over the steaks.

Note: Larger steaks can be prepared in the same way, but they will be more caloric.

Time: 10 minutes
Servings: 4
Calories: 325 per serving

VEAL PICCATA

- 2 tablespoons sweet (unsalted) butter
- 1/4 cup diced shallots
- 8 veal scaloppine (2 ounces each)
- 1/4 cup dry white wine
- 4 tablespoons chopped fresh Italian parsley leaves
  Juice of 2 lemons

1. Heat the butter in a large frying pan. Add the shallots and sauté for 2 minutes. Add the veal and sauté for 2 minutes on each side.

2. Add the lemon juice, wine, and parsley and cook 3 minutes longer, turning the veal pieces in the sauce to coat them well. Top with more fresh diced parsley and serve.

Time: 10 minutes
Servings: 4
Calories: 350 per serving

VEAL MOZZARELLA

1   large onion (3 ounces)
2   tablespoons vegetable oil
4   veal scaloppine (4 ounces each)
1/2 cup dry red wine
1   teaspoon Italian seasoning
4   slices part skim mozzarella, about 1 ounce each
2   tablespoons chopped fresh Italian parsley leaves

1. Peel and chop the onion.
2. Heat the oil in a large frying pan. Add the onion and sauté for 2 minutes. Add the veal and sauté for 3 minutes on each side.
3. Add the wine and Italian seasoning. Mix well and cook for 2 minutes.
4. Place 1 cheese slice on each scaloppine. Remove the pan from the heat and cover the pan for 2 minutes. Sprinkle each scaloppine with parsley when serving.

Time: 15 minutes
Servings: 4
Calories: 380 per serving

VEAL MARSALA WITH MUSHROOMS

This is good for simple and plain occasions, but it is also great for festive buffets.

    8 veal scaloppine (about 2 ounces each)
    1 cup fresh diced mushrooms
    2 shallots
  1/2 teaspoon Italian seasoning
    2 sprigs fresh Italian parsley leaves
  1/2 cup dry Marsala

1. Flatten the veal with the flat side of a cleaver to make very thin slices.
2. Slice the mushrooms.
3. Put the scaloppine in a large frying pan. Peel the shallots and chop them into the pan. Add the herbs, mushrooms, and wine. Bring the wine to a boil, lower the heat to a simmer, and cook the veal for 3 minutes on each side.
4. Simmer for a few minutes longer, or just until fruit is heated. Discard the parsley sprigs. Serve hot or cold.

Time: 10 minutes
Servings: 4
Calories: 295 per serving
Variation
    Instead of mushrooms, use 1/2 cup of sliced white grapes.

VEAL WITH SHRIMP AND ASPARAGUS

    8 fresh asparagus
   12 small shrimp
    2 tablespoons vegetable oil
    1 garlic clove, peeled
    3 shallots, peeled
  1/4 cup chopped fresh Italian parsley leaves
    8 veal scaloppine (about 2 ounces each)
  1/2 cup dry white wine
    3 tablespoons fresh lemon juice
       Lemon slices or wedges

1. Wash and trim the asparagus. Break off and discard all tough portions of the stems. Steam or blanch the asparagus for 5 minutes; they should still be green. Drain.

2. Shell and devein the shrimp. Poach the shrimp for 5 minutes; then drain.

3. Heat the oil in a large frying pan. Push the garlic through a press into the hot oil. Chop the shallots into the oil and add the parsley. Sauté until the shallots are translucent. Then add the veal scallops and sauté for 2 minutes on each side. Remove the veal to a serving platter or individual plates and keep warm.

4. Put the drained asparagus and shrimp in the frying pan and add the wine and lemon juice. Cook for a few minutes, then arrange 2 asparagus stalks and 3 shrimp on each veal scaloppine and spoon the sauce over all. Garnish with lemon slices or wedges and serve immediately.

Time: 20 minutes
Servings: 4
Calories: 350 per serving

VEAL SCALOPPINE PARMESAN

    8 veal scaloppine (about 2 ounces each)
    1/2 cup freshly grated Parmesan cheese
    1/2 cup minced fresh Italian parsley leaves
    1 tablespoon sweet (unsalted) butter
    1 tablespoon olive oil
    1/2 cup dry white wine

1. Pound the veal scallops with the flat side of a cleaver to make them thin.

2. Mix the cheese and parsley on a board or sheet of wax paper. Press each scaloppine into the mixture on both sides and press firmly to coat well. Let the scallops rest on another sheet of wax paper until ready to cook.

3. Heat the butter with oil in a large frying pan. Sauté the veal slices in a single layer for about 3 minutes on each side. (If necessary, do them in several batches, rather than crowding them.) Return all the scaloppine to the pan and add the wine. Simmer for a few minutes; then serve at once.

Time: 15 minutes
Servings: 4
Calories: 375 per serving

CHICKEN IN GARLIC SAUCE

4 boneless and skinless chicken breast halves (5 ounces each)
2 tablespoons extra virgin olive oil
4 garlic cloves, peeled
1/2 cup dry white wine
1/4 cup chopped fresh Italian parsley leaves

1. Rinse the chicken pieces and pat them dry.
2. Heat the oil in a large frying pan and push the garlic through a press into the hot oil. Add the chicken and sauté for 2 minutes on each side. Slash each piece so you can check the color.
3. Add the wine and bring to a boil. Lower the heat, cover the pan, and cook for 5 minutes, or until the color of the inside shows the chicken is done. Do not overcook. Sprinkle with parsley.

Variation
Sauté 1 cup sliced fresh mushrooms with the garlic and add to the chicken.

Time: 15 to 20 minutes
Servings: 4
Calories: 230 per serving

CHICKEN LIMONE

- 1 pound boneless and skinless chicken breast
- 1 tablespoon sweet (unsalted) butter
- 1/2 cup dry white wine
- 4 lemons

1. Rinse the chicken and pat it dry. Cut it into bite-sized pieces.

2. Melt the butter in a frying pan and add the chicken pieces. Sauté for 2 or 3 minutes, turning each piece once. Sprinkle lightly with salt and pepper; then add the wine and the juice of 2 of the lemons. Slice the remaining lemons into very thin slices, discarding any seeds, and add the slices to the pan. Cover the pan and simmer for 5 minutes. Serve hot or cold.

Time: 15 to 20 minutes
Servings: 4
Calories: 165 per serving

CHICKEN PARMA

8   small chicken parts (about 3 pounds total weight)
2   tablespoons vegetable oil
1   onion (4 ounces), peeled and chopped
1/2 cup chopped fresh mushrooms
1   cup dry white wine
1/4 cup chopped fresh Italian parsley leaves
1   teaspoon Italian seasoning
1/2 teaspoon snipped fresh or dried tarragon
6   tablespoons tomato paste
6   red Italian olives, pitted and sliced, or use ripe black olives

1. Remove the skin from the chicken pieces and rinse the pieces in cold water. Pat them dry.

2. Heat the oil in a large frying pan and brown the chicken pieces on all sides. Add the onion and mushrooms and sauté until the onion is translucent. Add the wine, half the parsley, the Italian seasoning, and tarragon. Simmer for 1 minute.

3. Add the tomato paste and olives, cover, and simmer for about 5 minutes, or until the chicken is cooked. If you have both white and dark meat, the dark may need an extra minute for tenderness, but be sure not to overcook the white meat pieces. Sprinkle with remaining parsley. Serve hot with noodles or rice.

Variation
Substitute dried mushrooms for the fresh mushrooms.

Time: 15 to 20 minutes
Servings: 8
Calories: 175 per serving, excluding noodles or rice

CHICKEN WITH HOT PEPPER SAUCE

    2 2 1/2-pound frying chickens
    1 dried tiny chili pepper or 1 teaspoon crushed red pepper
  1/2 pound ripe plum tomatoes
    3 tablespoons vegetable oil
1 1/2 cups dry white wine
  1/3 cup chopped fresh Italian parsley leaves

1. Cut the chickens into serving pieces; divide the breast halves into 2 portions. Save backs and necks for stock. Remove all the skin.

2. Wearing plastic or rubber gloves, slit the chili pepper and rinse away all the seeds. Cut out stem and any ribs. Still wearing the gloves, chop the pepper to fine bits.

3. Wash the tomatoes and core them. Chop the tomatoes. There should be about 1 cup. Put the chopped tomatoes in a sieve and let them drain.

4. Heat the oil in a large frying pan and sauté the chicken pieces until they are golden brown on all sides.

5. Pour the wine into the pan and simmer for a few minutes. Add the tomatoes, chopped chili pepper, and parsley.

6. Cover the pan, lower the heat, and cook for 10 minutes, or until the chicken is done to your taste.

Time: 25 minutes
Servings: 8
Calories: 260 per serving

PASTA, PASTA

TUNA AND TOMATO SAUCE FOR PASTA

This is good with green or white fettucine and ziti. The sauce can be cooked with rice instead of being served over it.

  1   7-ounce can water-packed tuna
  3   tablespoons grated lemon rind
1/2   pound ripe plum tomatoes
  2   tablespoons olive oil
  6   large shallots, peeled
1/4   cup chopped fresh Italian parsley leaves

1. Drain the tuna and mash it in a bowl. Sprinkle the lemon rind over the tuna (this counteracts any "fishy" taste).

2. Wash the tomatoes and remove the cores. Chop the tomatoes. There should be about 1 cup.

3. Heat the oil in a frying pan and chop the shallots into the pan. Sauté until the shallots are translucent.

4. Add the tomatoes and parsley and cook for 5 minutes, stirring.

5. Add the tuna with the lemon rind and cook for 2 minutes. Makes about 2 1/2 cups.

Time: 15 minutes
Servings: 10 (1/4 cup each)
Calories: 63 per 1/4 cup

FRITTATA WITH PASTA

6 eggs
1/3 cup freshly grated Parmesan cheese
1/4 cup chopped fresh Italian parsley leaves
1/3 teaspoon Italian seasoning
2 cups cooked pasta, cooked until just al dente (or any leftover pasta)
1 tablespoon plus 1 teaspoon vegetable oil
1/2 cup tomato sauce (page 191)
2 tablespoons freshly grated Parmesan cheese
6 sprigs fresh parsley

1. Beat the eggs in a large bowl and stir in the cheese, parsley, Italian seasoning, and pasta. Mix well.
2. Heat 1 tablespoon of the oil in a large frying pan and pour in the frittata mixture. Cook for 2 to 3 minutes, or until browned on the bottom.
3. Use the remaining oil to coat a plate slightly larger than the frying pan. Place it upside down on the pan and, holding pan and plate firmly together, turn them over.
4. Slide the frittata back into the pan with the uncooked side down. Cook for 2 or 3 minutes on the second side, then slide onto a serving plate.
5. Meanwhile, heat the sauce and pour it over the frittata. Garnish with additional cheese, if desired, and parsley sprigs.

Variations
Add diced cooked vegetables or small pieces of cooked chicken, turkey, ham, or ground beef to the beaten eggs.

Time: 15 minutes
Servings: 2
Calories: 340 per serving

LASAGNE WITH SPINACH AND CHEESE

1	pound lasagne noodles
1 1/2	pounds fresh spinach
1	pound ripe plum tomatoes
8	fresh mushrooms
8 to 10	shallots
2	tablespoons vegetable oil
1/4	cup chopped fresh Italian parsley leaves
1/4	teaspoon Italian seasoning
1/3	teaspoon freshly grated nutmeg
1	cup part skim ricotta
1/2	cup shredded part skim mozzarella

1. Fill a large pot with water and bring to a boil. Add salt and put in the lasagne noodles, one or two at a time, so the water does not stop boiling. Cook the noodles until they are cooked slightly less than *al dente*. Then carefully drain them and arrange them on a towel.

2. While noodles cook, prepare the sauce: Wash the spinach thoroughly. Then cook it in just the water clinging to the leaves for about 4 minutes. Lift the spinach from the saucepan to a colander and drain well. Chop the spinach. There should be 2 cups.

3. Wash the tomatoes and remove the cores. Chop the tomatoes. There should be 2 cups.

4. Wash and trim the mushrooms and chop them. There should be 1/2 cup.

5. Peel and mince the shallots. There should be 1/3 cup.

6. Heat the oil in a large frying pan and sauté the shallots and mushrooms until the shallots are translucent. Add the spinach, parsley, Italian seasoning, and nutmeg and continue to sauté for 2 minutes. Add the tomatoes and simmer, stirring often to mix well, for 5 minutes.

7. Preheat the oven to 350 degrees.

8. Spoon a thin layer of spinach sauce in the bottom of a deep 2-quart round baking dish. Then add a layer of noodles, another layer of spinach sauce, and about 1/4 cup of the ricotta and 2 tablespoons of mozzarella.

Continue in the same way, making 5 layers of noodles and sauce and 4 layers of the cheeses. Top the last layer of noodles and sauce with the mozzarella.

9. Bake for 8 to 10 minutes, or until done to your taste. Let the dish sit and cool slightly before cutting it into wedges.

Time: 30 minutes
Servings: 8
Calories: 350 per serving

MANICOTTI

1 pound manicotti shells (1 box)
2 cups part skim milk ricotta cheese
1/2 cup freshly grated Parmesan cheese
dash of pepper
Basic Tomato Sauce (page 189)

1. Prepare Tomato Sauce.
2. Cook the manicotti shells (undercooked, still firm). Rinse in cool water and carefully set on a working surface.
3. Use a large bowl and thoroughly mix the ricotta cheese with the Parmesan cheese and pepper.
4. Stuff the manicotti shells with ricotta mixture, enough to fill the entire shell but not beyond the end of the shells.
5. Place filled shells in a large baking pan and spoon tomato sauce over the manicotti and sprinkle with freshly grated Parmesan cheese.
6. Bake at 350° for 20 minutes. Serve warm.

Variations
Substitute for half the ricotta cheese an equal amount of chopped spinach. Use chopped meat or other vegetables. Also, cheese can be used instead of tomato sauce and topped with grated Parmesan cheese.

Time: 35 minutes
Servings: 4
Calories: 150 per filled manicotti shell

VEGETARIAN LASAGNE BRUNO

1 pound green lasagne noodles
1 pound fresh plum tomatoes or 3 cups canned imported
   Italian plum tomatoes
1/2 pound zucchini
1/2 pound eggplant
1 onion (2 ounces)
1 large sweet green pepper
3 tablespoons vegetable oil
1 garlic clove, peeled
1/2 teaspoon Italian seasoning
1/2 teaspoon hot red pepper flakes
1/2 cup freshly grated Parmesan cheese

1. Fill a large pot with water and bring to a boil. Put in the noodles, one or two at a time, so the water does not stop boiling. Cook the noodles until they are cooked slightly less than *al dente*. Then drain the noodles and carefully arrange them on a towel.

2. While the noodles cook, prepare the vegetables: Wash the tomatoes and remove the cores. Chop the tomatoes. There should be 2 cups.

3. Wash and trim the zucchini and eggplant and dice them. There should be 1 cup of each.

4. Peel and mince the onion and pepper.

5. Put the oil in a large frying pan and add the vegetables and garlic. Sauté, stirring a few times, for 5 minutes. Add the tomatoes, Italian seasoning, and hot pepper flakes, and cook for 10 minutes.

6. Preheat the oven to 350 degrees.

7. Spoon a little sauce in the bottom of a 2-quart lasagne dish and arrange a layer of lasagne noodles on top. Spoon some sauce over. Continue with more layers of noodles and sauce until the dish is filled. Sprinkle the cheese over the top.

8. Bake for 8 to 10 minutes, or until the dish is baked to your taste.

Time: 30 minutes
Servings: 8
Calories: 315 per serving

CLASSIC SEAFOOD SAUCE

- 1 tablespoon extra virgin olive oil
- 3 shallots, peeled
- 1 garlic clove, peeled
- 3 sprigs fresh Italian parsley
- 1/2 teaspoon hot red pepper flakes, optional
- 2 teaspoons Italian seasoning
- 1 cup chopped fresh seafood, such as shrimp, peeled calamari rings, steamed fresh tuna, shelled steamed mussels, or chopped fresh scallops
- 1/2 cup dry white wine

Heat the oil in a large saucepan. Chop the shallots and garlic into the hot oil. Snip in the parsley and add the red pepper flakes and Italian seasoning. Sauté over medium heat for a few minutes; then add the seafood and wine and cook for 3 minutes. Serve at once. Don't reheat this sauce as reheating will toughen the shrimp, calamari, mussels, and scallops. Makes about 1 1/2 cups.

Variation

For red sauce, add 1/2 cup chopped, peeled, and seeded fresh tomatoes when adding the seafood and wine.

Time: 6 to 10 minutes
Servings: 4 (6 tablespoons each)
Calories: 105 per 6 tablespoons

PASTA WITH ROASTED PEPPER SAUCE

 2 large sweet red peppers
 2 large sweet green peppers
 1 pound ripe plum tomatoes
 1 pound thin pasta or pennine (quills)
 1 onion (2 ounces)
 2 tablespoons olive oil
 1 garlic clove, peeled
1/3 cup chopped fresh Italian parsley leaves
   Cayenne pepper to taste

1. Roast the peppers over direct heat or under a broiler until the skin is browned. When they are cool enough to handle, peel off the skins, but do not wash the peppers. (Washing removes the roasted flavor that gives the character to the sauce.) If some blackened specks of peel remain on the peppers, it doesn't matter; they are edible. Discard the ribs and seeds and dice the peppers.

2. Wash the tomatoes and remove the cores. Chop the tomatoes.

3. Put the tomatoes and peppers in a blender container and reduce to a purée.

4. Fill a large pot with cold water. Bring to a boil over high heat. Add salt, if desired. Then add the pasta and cook, stirring occasionally, just until the pasta is *al dente*. Drain the pasta in a colander.

5. Peel and mince the onion.

6. While the pasta is cooking, heat the olive oil in a deep saucepan and push the garlic through a press into the hot oil. Add the onion and sauté until the onion is translucent. Add the pepper and tomato purée and the parsley and cayenne pepper and cook for 5 to 6 minutes. Add the pasta and toss it with the sauce.

Time: 20 minutes
Servings: 8
Calories: 270 per serving of pasta and sauce

FRITTATA

It is usual to say that a frittata is to the Italians like an omelette to the French, but actually a frittata is more flexible. This versatile dish can be used for nearly every course. It can be used as cocktail food by cutting the frittata into small squares. They can then be dipped into tomato, cheese, or vegetable sauce. Frittata makes an excellent first course served in wedges. For a first-course frittata mix the eggs with vegetables, seafood, chicken, meat, or cheese, or prepare it just plain. Serve a frittata as a main course, with all the fillings mentioned for a first course, and many varieties of sauces and toppings: cheese, tomato, vegetable purées, or chopped olives, almonds or herbs. Also, prepare a frittata like a pizza, with the sauce and filling on top, and sprinkle with Parmesan cheese; be sure to brown both sides slightly for this style.

1 to 2	tablespoons vegetable or olive oil
6	eggs
3	tablespoons water
5	tablespoons chopped fresh Italian parsley leaves
1/4	teaspoon Italian seasoning
1/2	cup filling (see Note)

1. Beat the eggs lightly with the water, parsley, and Italian seasoning. Add the filling and season with salt and pepper to taste. Blend thoroughly.

2. Pour enough of the oil into a large frying pan to cover the bottom. Heat the pan over low-to-medium heat. Pour in the egg mixture, making a layer about 1/2 inch thick. Cook for 3 or 4 minutes, or until the bottom is brown and firm. Shake the pan gently to prevent sticking.

3. Oil a plate slightly larger than the pan. Place it upside down on the pan and, holding pan and plate firmly together, turn them over. Slide the frittata back into the pan with the uncooked side down.

4. Continue to cook for a few minutes, until the underside is cooked to your taste. Turn out and serve. Or you can cover the skillet and continue cooking for a few minutes to set the top. Or slide the pan under the broiler

and cook for a few minutes until the top is finished to your taste.

Note: Good vegetables for the filling are mushrooms, onions, sweet green or red peppers, zucchini or other tender squashes. Cheese alone, or mixed with vegetables, is also good. All ingredients should be cut into fine slices or chopped or minced. They can be used raw if the time for cooking the frittata is enough time to cook the filling.

Variations
Serve with a topping of tomato sauce or cheese sauce. Serve with a vegetable mixture or purée spooned on top like Egg Foo Yung.
Sprinkle with grated Parmesan cheese or another cheese topping.

Time: 20 minutes
Servings: 4
Calories: 140 per serving

DESSERTS

BAKED FRUIT

Fruits to be baked whole should not be peeled; without the skin they lose their shape during baking.

    4 unpeeled medium-sized apples, pears, peaches, or nectarines
    6 tablespoons chopped or puréed fruit, or
    6 tablespoons part skim ricotta, mixed with 4 tablespoons
       Marsala
    1 cup water, mixed with 1/4 cup fresh lemon juice

1. Preheat the oven to 350 degrees.
2. Wash the fruit and remove the stem end. Remove the seed portion from the apples or with an apple corer or cut out the stones of the peaches or nectarines.
3. Fill the empty space with other fruits, chopped or puréed. Or fill with ricotta flavored with Marsala.
4. Put the stuffed fruits in a shallow baking dish and pour the lemon juice and water mixture over them. Bake for 10 minutes, or until the fruit reaches your desired tenderness. (The kind of fruit and the ripeness of the fruit will determine the cooking time. Apples will take longer than peaches, for instance.) Baste often during the baking time with the liquid in the bottom of the pan.

Time: 15 minutes
Servings: 4
Calories: 80 per serving

FROZEN ZABAGLIONE

3 eggs
1/4 cup sweet Marsala
1/4 cup prepared espresso coffee
2 teaspoons sugar

1. Separate the eggs.
2. Beat the yolks lightly; then add the Marsala and coffee and beat until well combined.
3. Beat the egg whites until they are frothy. Continue beating, gradually adding the sugar until stiff peaks form when the beaters are lifted. Gently fold the meringue into the egg-yolk mixture. Divide the mixture among 4 custard cups or other small dessert dishes and freeze until firm.

Time: 10 minutes, excluding time for freezing
Servings: 4
Calories: 90 per serving

FLOATING ISLAND IN AMARETTO SAUCE MARCO

1/4 cup fresh lemon juice
3 tablespoons water
2 7-gram envelopes unflavored gelatin
4 egg whites
1 teaspoon sugar
1/2 cup mixed finely sliced fresh fruit, such as apricots, oranges, peaches, and strawberries
1/4 cup Amaretto liqueur

1. Pour the lemon juice and water into a small saucepan. Sprinkle the gelatin on top and let it soften; then heat and stir until the gelatin dissolves. Cool.

2. Beat the egg whites until frothy. Continue beating, gradually adding the sugar until stiff peaks form when the beater is lifted.

3. Mix the fruit with the Amaretto. Stir the dissolved gelatin into the fruit; then gently fold the mixture into the meringue. (The lighter meringue will float to the top, making islands in the fruit sauce.)

4. Spoon into individual glasses and chill. Or pour into 4-cup baking dish and run under the broiler for a few minutes to brown the top; serve hot. Or serve as a sauce spooned over plain cake or ice cream.

Time: 15 minutes
Servings: 4
Calories: 110 per serving

STRAWBERRY-FILLED ORANGES

    4 navel oranges
    2 egg whites
    1 quart strawberries
    3 tablespoons Grand Marnier
    3 tablespoons fresh orange juice
    1 tablespoon grated orange rind
       Juice of 1 lemon
  1/2 teaspoon ground ginger

1. Cut the oranges into halves and remove the pulp. (Use the pulp for another recipe.)

2. Beat the egg whites lightly. Brush the inside of each orange shell with the beaten egg whites.

3. Wash and hull the strawberries and spoon them into the orange shells.

4. Mix the remaining ingredients together in a small bowl and divide evenly among the strawberry-filled orange halves. Chill.

Time: 15 minutes
Servings: 8 (1 orange half each)
Calories: 40 per orange half

Entertaining

I've created a special Entertainment Section to highlight today's perfect party food: the pasta salad. It never fails the test that such foods face because it is light, delicious, versatile, and absolutely festive-looking.

That's not to say that many of the menus and recipes in this book do not lend themselves to entertainment, too. (I like to think that Italian food always looks and tastes "festive.") However, the specially selected pasta salads are literally the pick of the crop, having been tested on friends and acquaintances who have given them rave reviews.

In addition to pasta salads, I've also included a few proven stand-by hits for the low-calorie party snack or dinner party. Try my Zucchini Stuffed with Meat or my always successful Timballo for your next dinner party.

PASTA SALAD CALIFORNIA

1 *pound short-shaped white pasta*
1/2 *pound fresh string beans*
3 *tablespoons vegetable oil*
1 *cup fresh mushrooms*
1 *cup part skim ricotta (or plain yogurt)*
  Pinch of dry mustard
1/2 *cup chopped fresh dill*
1/2 *cup walnuts, crushed*

1. Fill a large pot with cold water. Bring to a boil over high heat. Add salt, if desired. Then add the pasta and cook, stirring occasionally, just until the pasta is *al dente*. Drain the pasta in a colander and rinse it with cold water and drain again.
2. Dice and steam the string beans.
3. Toss the pasta with the oil and add the vegetables. Mix the ricotta with the mustard, dill, and walnuts and add to vegetables-pasta mixture. Chill before serving.

Variations
    Add diced pimientos or raisins.

Time: 10 minutes
Servings: 4
Calories: 320 per serving

PASTA SALAD ITALIA

  1 pound short white penne or ziti
  1 large eggplant
  3 tablespoons olive oil
  2 tablespoons red wine vinegar
  2 cups diced ripe tomatoes
  1/4 cup fresh chopped basil leaves
  1/4 teaspoon Italian seasoning
  1/4 cup chopped fresh Italian parsley leaves
  1 cup part skim ricotta

1. Fill a large pot with cold water. Bring to a boil over high heat. Add salt, if desired. Then add the pasta and cook, stirring occasionally, just until the pasta is *al dente*. Drain the pasta in a colander and rinse it with cold water and drain again.

2. Preheat the broiler.

3. Slice the eggplant in half and sprinkle it with 1 teaspoon oil and 1 teaspoon vinegar. Broil for 10 minutes. Then cool and dice it.

4. Toss the pasta with the oil and vinegar. Add diced tomatoes, basil, Italian seasoning, parsley, and eggplant. Season with salt and pepper to taste. Toss with the ricotta. Cover and chill.

Variations
    Add diced black olives and/or mushrooms.

Time: 20 minutes
Servings: 4
Calories: 460 per serving

PASTA SALAD WITH CURRIED CHICKEN

1 pound green and white swirl-shaped pasta
2 cups chicken breast, cooked
2 tablespoons vegetable oil
1 cup plain yogurt
1 teaspoon curry powder
1 cup fresh, soft mango, diced, optional
1/2 cup diced sweet red pepper
1/4 cup diced celery
3 tablespoons sesame seeds

1. Fill a large pot with cold water. Bring to a boil over high heat. Add salt, if desired. Then add the pasta and cook, stirring occasionally, just until the pasta is *al dente*. Drain the pasta in a colander and rinse it with cold water and drain again.

2. Sauté the chicken breast in vegetable oil and cut it into 1/4-inch cubes.

3. Mix the yogurt and curry powder together.

4. Put the pasta in a large bowl and toss with the chicken, mango, diced pepper, diced celery, and yogurt sauce. Sprinkle with the sesame seeds. Cover and chill.

Variations
Substitute diced kiwi, papaya, or pineapple for the mango.

Time: 25 minutes
Servings: 4
Calories: 450 (yogurt)

PASTA SALAD PEKING

>   1 pound Chinese noodles, such as bean thread noodles,
>   cellophane noodles, somen, or rice noodles
>   2 cups diced broccoli flowerets
>   1 cup diced sweet red pepper
>   1 cup diced asparagus tips
> 1/2 pound snow peas
>   3 tablespoons safflower oil
>   1 teaspoon hot red pepper flakes, or 1/2 teaspoon cayenne
>   pepper
>   1 teaspoon grated fresh ginger
>   2 cloves garlic, peeled

1. Soak the Chinese noodles in cold water until tender.
2. Sauté the diced vegetables in 2 tablespoons of oil.
3. Toss the noodles and snow peas with the remaining oil and the hot pepper flakes; then add the vegetables, garlic, and ginger and toss again. Serve at room temperature.

Variations
    Add sliced zucchini and/or mushrooms or chopped chestnuts to the salad.

Time: 30 minutes
Servings: 4
Calories: 280 per serving

PASTA SALAD ATHENA

1   pound ziti, mixed green and white
3   tablespoons olive oil
2   tablespoons red wine vinegar
1   cup diced black olives
1/2   cup diced onions
1   cup diced tomatoes
1   large sweet green pepper, diced
1   head Boston lettuce, broken into small pieces
1/2   teaspoon Italian seasoning
1   cup crumbled feta cheese

1. Fill a large pot with cold water. Bring to a boil over high heat. Add salt, if desired. Then add the pasta and cook, stirring occasionally, just until the pasta is *al dente*. Drain the pasta in a colander and rinse it with cold water and drain again.

2. Toss the pasta with the oil and add all the remaining ingredients, except the feta cheese. Toss again.

3. Sprinkle with feta cheese before serving.

Variation
Add sliced mushrooms and zucchini.

Time: 15 minutes
Servings: 4
Calories: 400

SEAFOOD PASTA SALAD

>   1 *pound small pasta shapes*
>   1 1/2 *pounds fresh- or saltwater fish fillets*
>   1/2 *pound ripe plum tomatoes*
>   1/2 *cup chopped shallots*
>   1/4 *cup chopped fresh Italian parsley leaves*
>   2 *garlic cloves, peeled*
>   1 *tablespoon olive oil*
>   1/4 *cup fresh lemon juice*
>   2 *tablespoons drained capers*
>   2 *bay leaves*

1. Fill a large pot with cold water. Bring to a boil over high heat. Add salt, if desired. Then add the pasta and cook, stirring occasionally, just until the pasta is *al dente*. Drain the pasta in a colander and rinse it with cold water and drain again. Transfer the pasta to a bowl and toss it with the oil. Chill until needed.

2. Cut the fish into 1-inch cubes and poach them in a small amount of water for 6 minutes. Drain and cool.

3. Wash the tomatoes and remove the core. Chop the tomatoes. There should be 1 cup.

4. Put the tomatoes into a large mixing bowl and add the shallots and parsley. Push the garlic through a press into the bowl. Add the fish cubes and olive oil and toss gently to mix. Add the lemon juice, capers, bay leaves, and salt and pepper to taste. Cover and chill.

5. Toss the salad with the chilled pasta. Remove the bay leaves before serving.

Variation

Heat the oil in a frying pan and push the garlic through a press into the hot oil. Add the shallots and chopped tomatoes. Cook for 5 minutes. Add the parsley, lemon juice, capers, bay leaves, and fish cubes. Cook for 5 minutes, or until the fish is just tender. Season with salt and pepper to taste. Remove the bay leaves and serve warm.

Time: 15 minutes, excluding time for chilling

Servings: 6

Calories: 160 per serving (based on striped bass)

ZUCCHINI STUFFED WITH MEAT

6	*medium-sized zucchini (about 6 ounces each)*
6 to 8	*shallots*
6	*large fresh mushrooms*
1 1/2	*tablespoons olive oil*
1	*teaspoon hot red pepper flakes*
1/2	*pound ground lean beef, veal, or chicken*
3	*tablespoons chopped fresh Italian parsley leaves*
2	*tablespoons dry red wine*
1	*egg yolk*
2	*tablespoons chopped drained pimiento*
1	*tablespoon freshly grated Parmesan cheese*

1. Scrub and trim the zucchini, but do not peel them. Cut each one lengthwise into halves and carefully scoop out the pulp without damaging the shells. Cover the shells with cold water, bring to a boil, and boil for 2 minutes. Then drain and plunge into cold water. Drain the shells upside down while preparing the stuffing.

2. Peel and chop the shallots. There should be 1/3 cup. Wash and trim the mushrooms and chop them. There should be 1/3 cup.

3. Heat 1 tablespoon of the oil in a frying pan and sauté the zucchini pulp, shallots, mushrooms, and hot pepper flakes until the shallots are translucent. Add the ground meat, half of the parsley, and the red wine. Sauté for 2 minutes, or until the meat is cooked. Season the stuffing with salt and pepper to taste.

4. Preheat the oven to 350 degrees.

5. Beat the egg yolk slightly and brush some on the inside of each zucchini boat. Fill the boats with the meat stuffing. Top each filled shell with bits of pimiento and a pinch of cheese.

6. Use the rest of the oil to coat a shallow baking pan. Place the zucchini shells in the pan and bake for 10 minutes, or until done to your taste. Sprinkle the remaining parsley on top before serving.

Variations

Substitute chopped black olives or anchovies for the mushrooms.

Use tomato sauce instead of the wine.

Time: 25 to 30 minutes

Servings: 6 (2 halves per serving)

Calories: 72 per zucchini half

TIMBALLO

A timballo is a dish similar to lasagne, but it is made in a round baking dish and cut into wedges like a pie. Usually it has many more layers than lasagne, and is much higher. In Italy, the noodles are made at home (pasta fresca) and they are very thin and tender. You can use the packaged lasagne noodles and cut off the curved edge after cooking. Or instead of using noodles, make the timballo with vegetable pancakes layered with the sauce or filling. Try this method with this delicious zucchini pancake recipe.

ZUCCHINI PANCAKES

    4 small zucchini (about 4 ounces each)
    3 eggs
    1/4 cup water
    1/4 cup whole wheat flour
    3 tablespoons chopped fresh Italian parsley leaves
    2 tablespoons vegetable oil

1. Wash and peel the zucchini and cut them into small pieces. Purée the zucchini in a blender.

2. Beat the eggs lightly in a bowl and add the zucchini, water, flour, and parsley.

3. Return the mixture to the blender and whirl for a few seconds, or until well mixed. (The batter does not need to be as smooth as cream.) For the best results, let the batter rest in a cool place for 1 hour, but this is not essential.

4. Brush a 5-inch frying pan with a few drops of the oil and heat the pan until a drop of water skips across the pan. Spoon 3 tablespoons of the batter into the pan and quickly turn and tip the pan so the batter covers the entire surface. Cook until the top shows little holes and the bottom is lightly browned, just a few minutes. Flip the pancake over and brown the other side. Remove to a plate and keep warm. Continue to brush the pan with a few drops of the oil and make pancakes until all the batter is used.

Variations

To make less of a pancake and more of a frittata, omit the whole wheat flour and add 3 more eggs (which will increase the calories). Serve the little frittatas plain or filled.

Fill the pancakes or frittatas with seafood, vegetable mixtures, meat sauce, rice and chicken, mushrooms and mozzarella cheese, and roll up like crêpes. Or make layers as if making a layer cake, and serve cut into wedges.

Top either pancakes or frittatas with tomato sauce and cheese.

Time: 10 to 15 minutes, excluding time to rest the batter
Servings: approximately 16
Calories: 40 per pancake

CALORIES OF MOST-USED FOODS

FOOD	AMOUNT	CALORIES
alcoholic beverages		
beer	12 ounces	150 to 170
distilled spirits (bourbon, gin, Scotch, vodka)	1 ounce, 80 to 100 proof	75 to 85
liqueurs		
brandy	1 ounce	80
Grand Marnier	1 ounce	100
Maraschino	1 ounce	94
Tia Maria, Kahlua	1 ounce	92
wine		
champagne, dry	4 ounces	100 to 115
Marsala, dry	4 ounces	160
Marsala, sweet	4 ounces	200
vermouth, dry	4 ounces	135
red wine, dry	4 ounces	95 to 100
white wine, dry	4 ounces	85 to 95
anchovy	1 fillet	7
apple	1 unpeeled apple, 5 ounces	80
artichoke	1 fresh artichoke, 8 ounces	35
	3 frozen hearts	22
asparagus	1 pound raw	66
beans		
string or wax	1/2 cup cooked fresh beans	16
Italian	1/2 cup cooked fresh beans	45
beef		
chuck	3 1/2 ounces, lean, braised	265
club steak	3 1/2 ounces, lean, broiled	280
ground beef	3 1/2 ounces, lean, broiled	220
round, bottom	3 1/2 ounces, lean, broiled	240
steak, lean	3 1/2 ounces raw	164
boullion cube	1 cube	5
bread		
cracked wheat	1 slice	60
Italian	1 slice, 1-inch thick	55

FOOD	AMOUNT	CALORIES
white	1 slice	70
whole wheat	1 slice	55
broccoli	1 pound raw	113
	1/2 cup cooked fresh	25
butter	1 tablespoon	100
carrot	1/2 pound raw	80
cauliflower	1/2 pound raw	60
celery	1 cup diced raw	15
cheese		
cottage or ricotta	part skim, 1/2 cup	80
mozzarella	1 ounce	80
Parmesan or Pecorino	1 tablespoon grated	30
chicken		
breast	3 1/2 ounces raw	100
	3 1/2 ounces, without skin, broiled or poached	135
dark meat	3 1/2 ounces, roasted	180
white meat	3 1/2 ounces, roasted	165
clams	3 1/2 ounces fresh meats, no shells	82
	3 1/2 ounces canned meats, drained	98
cod	3 1/2 ounces fresh, without skin or bones	78
	3 1/2 ounces salted	130
cornstarch	1 tablespoon	30
crab	3 1/2 ounces fresh meat, no shells	93
	3 1/2 ounces canned	101
crackers		
graham	1 medium-sized cracker	28
saltine	1 saltine	22
Venus Wheat Wafers	1 wafer	18

FOOD	AMOUNT	CALORIES
cream, light	1 tablespoon	45
cream, sour	1 tablespoon	30
egg	1 whole large egg	80
	1 large egg white	15
	1 large egg yolk	60
eggplant	3 1/2 ounces raw	25
	1/2 cup simmered pieces	19
endive and escarole	3 1/2 ounces raw	20
flounder	3 1/2 ounces fresh	79
flour		
whole wheat	3 1/2 ounces hard wheat	333
enriched all-purpose	3 1/2 ounces	364
garlic	1 clove, 3 grams	3
gelatin	1 envelope, 7 grams, unflavored	28
gingerroot	1/2 ounce fresh	50
grapefruit	1 cup fresh sections	75
grapes	1 cup raw seedless green grapes	95
haddock	3 1/2 ounces fresh	80
halibut	3 1/2 ounces fresh	100
honey	1 tablespoon	64
lamb		
leg	3 1/2 ounces lean, roasted, without bone	195
loin chop	5 ounces, lean, with bone	225
rib chop	5 ounces, lean, with bone	325
shoulder	3 1/2 ounces, lean, roasted, without bone	220
leek	1 large raw	17

OOD	AMOUNT	CALORIES
lemon	1 tablespoon fresh juice	4
lettuce		
iceberg	1/2 pound raw	28
loose leaf	1/2 pound raw	26
romaine	1/2 pound raw	26
liver		
beef	3 1/2 ounces raw	125
	3 1/2 ounces broiled	180
calf's	3 1/2 ounces raw	140
	3 1/2 ounces broiled	220
chicken	3 1/2 ounces raw	110
lobster		
American	3 1/2 ounces raw meat	91
spiny	3 1/2 ounces raw meat	72
milk		
skim	1 cup, 8 ounces	90
whole	1 cup, 8 ounces	160
mushrooms	1/2 pound raw	60
mussels	3 1/2 ounces fresh meats, no shells	66
mustard	1 tablespoon prepared	11
oil		
olive	1 tablespoon	130
vegetable	1 tablespoon	125
onion	1/2 pound raw	80
	1 onion, 3 ounces	30
	1 tablespoon chopped raw	4
	1/2 cup chopped raw	32
orange	1 Florida orange, 7 ounces	75
	1 California orange, 6 ounces	60
oysters	3 1/2 ounces fresh meat of Eastern oysters, no shells	66
parsley	1 tablespoon raw chopped	2

FOOD	AMOUNT	CALORIE*
pasta	2 ounces uncooked	21
macaroni	1/2 cup cooked *al dente*, with no sauce	7
noodles	1/2 cup cooked *al dente*, with no sauce	10
spaghetti	1/2 cup cooked *al dente*, with no sauce	9
peach	1 fresh peach, 4 ounces	3
pear	1 fresh pear, 7 ounces	10
peas, fresh green	1/2 cup cooked	5
pepper, sweet bell	1 green pepper, 5 ounces	2
	1 red pepper, 5 ounces	3
pignolis (pine nuts)	1 tablespoon	5
pimiento	1 canned	1
pineapple	1/2 cup diced fresh	3
	3 1/2 ounces canned, packed in natural juices	5
potato	1 potato, 3 1/2 ounces, raw	7
	1 potato, 3 1/2 ounces, peeled and boiled	6
quail	3 1/2 ounces raw, without skin and bones	16
rabbit	3 1/2 ounces raw, without skin and bones	16
radishes	3 1/2 ounces, 1 cup, raw, about 15 small radishes	2
raisins	1/2 cup	23
raspberries	1/2 cup fresh raw	3
rice		
white, long-grain	3 1/2 ounces raw	36
	1/2 cup cooked	92
brown	3 1/2 ounces raw	36
	1/2 cup cooked	10

FOOD	AMOUNT	CALORIES
...gola	1/2 pound raw	50
...lmon	3 1/2 ounces fresh	220
	3 1/2 ounces, poached	210
	4 ounces, canned	160 to 240
...rdines	3 1/2 ounces fresh	160
	3 1/2 ounces canned in brine, drained	196
	3 1/2 ounces canned in oil, drained	205
...allions	6 scallions without tops	20
...allops	3 1/2 ounces fresh	81
...allots	1 ounce	18
...rimp	3 1/2 ounces fresh, no shells	91
	3 1/2 ounces canned, drained	116
...apper	3 1/2 ounces, fresh, without skin or bones	90
...ft drinks		
club soda	8 ounces	0
cola	8 ounces	95
ginger ale	8 ounces	85
...le	3 1/2 ounces fresh, without skin or bones	79
...inach	3 1/2 ounces raw	26
	1/2 cup boiled, drained	21
...quash		
yellow summer	3 1/2 ounces raw	20
...quash		
	1/2 cup cooked, drained	16
zucchini	3 1/2 ounces raw	17
	1/2 cup cooked, drained	13
...quid	3 1/2 ounces fresh meat	84
...ock		
chicken	1 cup (homemade)	30
veal	1 cup (homemade)	35
vegetable	1 cup (homemade)	10

FOOD	AMOUNT	CALORI
strawberries	3 1/2 ounces fresh raw, about 2/3 cup	
striped bass	3 1/2 ounces fresh raw, without skin or bones	1
sugar		
brown	1 tablespoon	
white	1 tablespoon	
tomato paste	canned, 1 tablespoon	
tomato purée	canned, 1/4 cup	
tomatoes		
cherry tomatoes	1 cup	
plum tomatoes	1 tomato, 8 to 1 pound	
	canned, 1/2 cup	
round tomatoes	1 tomato, 3 to 1 pound	
trout	3 1/2 ounces fresh brook trout	1
tuna	3 1/2 ounces canned in oil, undrained	2
	3 1/2 ounces canned in water, undrained	1
turkey	3 1/2 ounces raw white meat, without skin or bones	1
	3 1/2 ounces roasted white meat, without skin or bones	1
veal		
loin chop	6 ounces with bone, raw	2
scallop (scaloppine)	1 scallop, 2 ounces	1
shoulder or rump	3 1/2 ounces, with no fat	1
vinegar	1 tablespoon	
watercress	3 1/2 ounces raw 5 sprigs	
Worcestershire sauce	1 tablespoon	
yogurt	1 cup, lowfat, plain	1

Index

From Very Famous Chefs

__BARBECUE WITH BEARD
James Beard   (Z35-062, $2.75)

This outdoor cookbook shows you how to turn out master-pieces every time. Every method of outdoor cooking is explored from a charcoal hibachi to an electric rotisserie. There are recipes for every main course from hamburgers to Chateaubriand—and for the accompaniments from dip to dessert. It's a gallery of good things to eat presented by the master himself.

__JAMES BEARD'S FISH COOKERY
James Beard   (Z32-948, $4.95, U.S.A.)
                                       (Z32-949, $6.25, Canada)

From halibut and salmon to grunion and pompano, trout to buffalo fish, or abalone to conch and oysters: James Beard has all the valuable information about how to choose and cook fish. Hundreds of delicious recipes makes this "a must for any good cook's collection."   —*Dallas Times Herald*

__MAIDA HEATTER'S BOOK OF GREAT DESSERTS
Maida Heatter   (Z30-710, $4.95)

Maida Heatter brings you her very best recipes in this book. From the easy-to-make Raspberry Strawberry Bavarian to the super-sophisticated Dobosh Torte, each recipe is accompanied by clear, step-by-step directions to insure that each comes out exactly as it should. Nothing is left vague. She tells you exactly where the racks should be placed in the oven, when and how to test, at what speed to set the electric beater—even how to improvise, if you must.

WARNER BOOKS
P.O. Box 690
New York, N.Y. 10019

Please send me the books I have checked. I enclose a check or money order (not cash), plus 50¢ per order and 50¢ per copy to cover postage and handling.* (Allow 4 weeks for delivery.)

_____ Please send me your free mail order catalog. (If ordering only the catalog, include a large self-addressed, stamped envelope.)

Name _____

Address _____

City _____

State _____ Zip _____

*N.Y. State and California residents add applicable sales tax.   87